BRITISH GENEALOGICAL PERIODICALS
A BIBLIOGRAPHY OF THEIR CONTENTS

VOLUME 1

COLLECTANEA TOPOGRAPHICA ET GENEALOGICA
TOPOGRAPHER AND GENEALOGIST
ANCESTOR

— BY —
STUART RAYMOND

FEDERATION OF FAMILY HISTORY SOCIETIES

Published by the
Federation of Family History Societies,
c/o The Benson Room, Birmingham and Midland Institute,
Margaret Street, Birmingham B3 3BS, England.

Copies also obtainable from
S.A. and M.J. Raymond, 6 Russet Avenue, Heavitree, Exeter EX1 3QB, U.K.
S.A. and M.J. Raymond, P.O. Box 255, Belmont, Vic. 3216, Australia.

Printed by Parchment (Oxford) Limited.

Acknowledgments

This bibliography was compiled using the resources of the State Library of Victoria, in Melbourne, Australia, Exeter University Library, and the Devon and Exeter Institution, and I am grateful to the librarians of these institutions for enabling me to gain access to their collections. I am also grateful for the assistance of my wife, Marjorie, who has done much of the work of typing and indexing.

Stuart A. Raymond

Cataloguing in publication data:

Raymond, Stuart A., 1945-
British genealogical periodicals: a bibliography of their contents.
Vol. 1: Collectanea topographica et genealogica; Topographer and genealogist; Ancestor.
British genealogical bibliographies.
Birmingham, England: Federation of Family History Societies, 1991.

DDC 016.92910941

ISBN 1 872094 20 1

ISSN: 1033-2065

CONTENTS

COLLECTANEA TOPOGRAPHICA ET GENEALOGICA

8 volumes

London: John Bowyer Nichols and Son, 1834-1843

with

TOPOGRAPHER AND GENEALOGIST

3 Volumes

London: John Bowyer Nichols and Son, 1846-1858

COLLECTANEA TOPOGRAPHICA ET GENEALOGICA

with

TOPOGRAPHER AND GENEALOGIST

INTRODUCTION

John Gough Nicholls' Collectanea topographica et genealogica, which was continued by the Topographer and genealogist, was one of the earliest genealogical journals, commencing in 1834. Eight volumes were published up to 1843, followed by three volumes of the Topographer and genealogist, 1846-1858. It included many family histories and pedigrees; however, its strength lay in its many extracts from records such as parish registers, monumental inscriptions, wills, deeds, etc..

The purpose of this bibliography is to assist researchers in identifying material relevant to their research. The names of authors, and the titles of articles, are given in full. An attempt has been made to indicate the county and period to which an article pertains, if this information is not included in the title.

In addition to the present bibliography, each volume of Collectanea topographica et genealogica and Topographer and genealogist has extensive indexes of matters, places, and persons.

Stuart A. Raymond

1. BIRTHS, MARRIAGES AND DEATHS

LE NEVE, Peter. 'Memoranda in heraldry', T.G., 3, 1858, p.25-48, 147-54, 261-9, 375-84, & 504-11. [Principally notes of deaths and funerals]

M. 'Genealogical and historical notes from ancient calendars, &c', C.T.G., 1, 1834, p.277-83; 2, 1835, p.174-8 & 368-87; 3, 1836, p.376-80; 6, 1840, p.90-98. [Medieval records of births, marriages and deaths]

P 'Extracts from a volume of Robert Aske's collections, marked with a cinquefoil, written in the reign of Henry VIII', C.T.G., 1, 1834, p.20-23, 168-70, 243-8 & 324-30. [{Pt. 1.} List of medieval burials at Clare, Harlyng, and the Chapter House of London; marriages in the royal presence; pedigree of Broke (late medieval). {Pt. 2.} Burials at Lanthony; medieval pedigree of Fleming, Camefelde and Haveryngton; burials at Gisborough Priory, Yorkshire. {Pt.3.} Descendants of Matthew Furneaux of Bytton, Co. Somerset. {Pt.4.} Pedigree of Danvers of Cotherop, Co. Oxon, including descents of Umpton, Englefield, Tracy, Gate, Fray, Walgrave, Power, Langstone, Boteler, Gifford, Fowler, Chamberlain, &c &c; Pedigree of Fitzwarine of Staffordshire]

BEDFORDSHIRE

Campton

G., H. H. 'Extracts from the parish registers and epitaphs at Campton, Co. Bedford', C.T.G., 3, 1836, p.121-31.

Cople

W., E. R. 'Extracts from the register of Cople, Co. Bedford, chiefly relating to the family of Luke', C.T.G., 5, 1838, p.362-5.

Hawnes

G., H. H. 'Extracts from the parish registers, and epitaphs, at Hawnes, Co. Bedford', C.T.G., 3, 1836, p.85-8.

BERKSHIRE

Welford

W., J. 'Extracts from the registers of Welford, Berks., and Hungerford and Bedwyn Parva, Wilts., chiefly relating to the family of Hungerford', C.T.G., 5, 1838, p.359-62.

BUCKINGHAMSHIRE

Burnham

N., J. G. 'Church notes of Burnham, Co. Buckingham, by the Rev. William Cole, F. S. A', C.T.G., 4, 1837, p.265-304. [Includes parish register extracts, list of rectors and vicars, monumental inscriptions, etc.]

Iver

N., J. G. 'Extracts from the parish register of Iver, in Buckinghamshire', C.T.G., 3, 1836, p.279-84.

CHESHIRE

Backford

G., S. 'Extracts from the parish registers of Backford, in the county of Chester', C.T.G., 4, 1837, p.232.

Farndon

G., S. 'Extracts from the registers of the parish of Farndon, Co. Chester, commencing 1601', C.T.G., 4, 1837, p.233-8.

DORSET

Sutton Waldron

W., J. 'Extracts from the registers of Sutton Waldron, near Shaftesbury, Dorset', T.G., 3, 1858, p.411-13.

ESSEX

Theydon Mount

G., G. 'Extracts from the parish registers of Theydon Mount, Essex, which begins 1564', C.T.G., 8, 1843, p.406-8.

GLOUCESTERSHIRE

Ashton-sub-Edge

B., J. 'Description of an ancient register of the parish of Ashton-sub-Edge, Co. Gloucester, with extracts', C.T.G., 7, 1841, p.279-85. [from 1539]

KENT

Down

S., G. S. 'Extracts from the parish register of Down, Co. Kent', T.G., 2, 1853, p.280-4 & 532-4.

LONDON AND MIDDLESEX

B., J. S. 'Registers of private chapels in and near London', C.T.G., 3, 1836, p.381-9. [Includes register transcripts from Duke Street Chapel, Westminster, the Rolls Chapel, St. John's Chapel, Bedford Row, and Wheeler Chapel, Spitalfields, 17-18th c.]

B., J. S. 'Further account of registers of private chapels in and near London', C.T.G., 4, 1837, p.157-64. [Gray's Inn Chapel; Knightsbridge chapel; 17-18th c.]

Charterhouse

Y., C. G. 'Burials in the Charterhouse, London', C.T.G., 4, 1837, p.308-10. [Late medieval]

Hammersmith

N., J. G. 'Extracts from the registers of Hammersmith, Co. Middlesex', C.T.G., 3, 1836, p.316-20.

St. Dunstan's in the West

N., J. G. 'Extracts from the parish registers of St. Dunstan's in the West, London', C.T.G., 5, 1838, p.202-20 & 365-84. See also below, p.14.

St. Olave, Hart Street.

G., H. H. Extracts from the parish registers of St. Olave, Hart Street, London', C.T.G., 2, 1835, p.311-7.

Westminster Abbey

M. 'Expenses of ancient funeral hearses at Westminster Abbey', C.T.G., 3, 1836, p.380-1. [Medieval]

Y., C. G. 'Register of baptisms in Westminster Abbey', C.T.G., 7, 1841, p.243-8.

Y., C. G. 'Register of burials in Westminster Abbey', C.T.G., 7, 1841, p.355-77; 8, 1843, p.1-23.

Y., C. G. 'Register of marriages in Westminster Abbey', C.T.G., 7, 1841, p.162-74.

'Burials in Westminster Abbey', C.T.G., 8, 1843, p. 152-4. [Order for dis-interment and re-burial of Parliamentarians, 1661]

Westminster, St. James

ADAMS, G. E. 'Extracts from the parish register of St. James, Westminster', T.G., 3, 1858, p.491-503. [These extracts were not continued in T.G., despite the promise that they would be]

NORTHAMPTONSHIRE

Chacombe

'Burials at Chacombe Priory, Co. Northampton', C.T.G., 2, 1835, p.388-9. [Medieval]

Great Billington

Y., C. G. 'Extracts from the register of the parish of Great Billington, Co. Northampton, chiefly relating to the family of O'Brien, Earls of Thomond', C.T.G., 8, 1843, p.189-90.

SURREY

Addington

S., G. S. 'Extracts from the registers of Addington, Co. Surrey', C.T.G., 7, 1841, p.286-91.

Camberwell

S., G. S. 'Extracts from the parish registers of Camberwell, Surrey', C.T.G., 3, 1836, p.142-68.

Croydon

S., G. S. 'Extracts from the parish registers of Croydon, Surrey', C.T.G., 2, 1835, p.292-6. [Includes a few monumental inscriptions]

S., G. S. 'Further extracts from the parish registers of Croydon', C.T.G., 3, 1836, p.307-8; 4, 1837, p.91-5.

Streatham

N., J. G. 'Extracts from the parish register of Streatham, Co. Surrey', C.T.G., 3, 1836, p.309-13.

WILTSHIRE

Aldbourne

L., C. E. 'Extracts from the parish register of Aldbourne, North Wilts., with a few church notes, and genealogical particulars', C.T.G., 6, 1840, p.385-91.

Bedwyn Parva

See under Berkshire. Welford

Burbage

See Collingbourne Ducis

Chilton Foliot

W., J. 'Church-notes, and extracts from the parish registers, of Chilton Foliot, Co. Wilts', T.G., 3, 1858, p.575-91.

Chute

W., J. 'Extracts from the parish registers of Chute and Market Lavington, in the county of Wilts', C.T.G., 8, 1843, p. 190-204.

Collingbourne Ducis and Collingbourne Kingston

W., J. 'Extracts from the registers of Collingbourne Ducis, Collingbourne Kingston, Burbage, and Tidcombe, Co. Wilts', C.T.G., 7, 1841, p.72-80.

W., J. 'Extracts from the parish registers of Collingbourne Kingston, Burbage, and Tidcombe, Wilts', C.T.G., 7, 1841, p.175-90.

Hungerford

See under Berkshire. Welford

Malmesbury

THOMAS, B. C. 'Extracts from the parish register of Malmesbury, Co. Wilts', C.T.G., 6, 1840, p.237-44.

Market Lavington

See Chute

Marlborough

W., J. 'Extracts from the registers of the parishes of St. Peter and St. Paul the apostles, and St. Mary the Virgin, Marlborough, with the most important of unpublished epitaphs', C.T.G., 5, 1838, p.260-74.

Mildenhall

See Preshute

Milton Lislebon

W., J. 'Extracts from the parish registers of Milton Lislebon, near Pewsey, Co. Wilts', T.G., 3, 1858, p.347-52.

Ogbourne St. Andrew and Ogbourne St. George

See Preshute

Preshute

W., J. 'Extracts from the registers of Preshute, Mildenhall, Ogbourne St. Andrew and Ogbourne St. George, Wilts., with some of the most important and unpublished epitaphs', C.T.G., 5, 1838, p.346-59.

Tidcombe

See Collingbourne Ducis

YORKSHIRE

Y., C. G. 'Notices concerning religious houses in Yorkshire, with the names of their founders, and of persons buried therein', C.T.G., 4, 1837, p.73-80 & 128-33.

Gisburne

Y., C. G. 'Patrons of Wynestead, Co. York. Obits in the register of Gisburne Priory. Births of the Mowbrays. Lords of Harewood, Co. York. Inquisitions of the Daunays', C.T.G., 4, 1837, p.261-4. [Medieval]

Hornby

W., J. 'Extracts from the parish registers of Hornby, Co. York', T.G., 3, 1858, p.325-47.

Tong

Y., C. G. ' 'Extracts from the registers of the church of Tong, in the parish of Birstall, in the West Riding of the county of York, relative to the family of Tempest', C.T.G., 8, 1843, p.364-8.

Wath

W., J. 'Extracts from the parish registers of Wath, near Ripon', T.G., 3, 1858, p.414-36. See corrigenda, p.591-6.

IRELAND

Dublin

D'Alton, John, 'Extracts from the parish registers of Saint Nicholas, Dublin', T.G., 2, 1853, p.520-31.

2. MONUMENTAL INSCRIPTIONS

A. OVERSEAS

BRUGES

S., G. S. 'English epitaphs at Bruges', T.G., 2, 1853, p.535-9. [Letter to the editor, noting additions and corrections to the following articles]

S., G. S. 'Sepulchral memorials of the English at Bruges', T.G., 2, 1853, p.137-52.

STEINMAN, G. Steinman. 'Sepulchral monuments of the English formerly at Bruges, extracted from the ms. "X Sepultur der stad Brugge" in the Bibliotheque Publique at Bruges', T.G., 2, 1853, p.468-93.

PARIS

J., H. L. 'Sepulchral inscriptions at the Convent of Canonesses Regular of the order of St. Augustines, Rue Des Fosses, St. Victor, Paris', C.T.G., 8, 1843, p.24-31.

J., H. L. 'Sepulchral inscriptions in the chapel of the Irish College at Paris', C.T.G., 7, 1841, p.111-7.

SHIRLEY, Ev. Ph. 'Epitaphs in the Huguenot's burying place at Paris, 1675', T.G., 3, 1858, p.298-301. [Monumental inscriptions to Robert & Ingram Rich, Ralph Crewe, Thomas Spencer, Richard Steward, Henrietta Cornwallis, John Godfrey, & Stephen Fox]

'Sepulchral inscriptions at the Scotch College, Paris', C.T.G., 6, 1840, p.32-41.

ROME

TREVELYAN, W. C. 'Names of pilgrims from England to Rome in the years 1504-1507, 1581-1587, with some of earlier date', C.T.G., 5, 1838, p.62-88. [Includes monumental inscriptions and list of wills, 14-18th c.]

B. ENGLAND

BEDFORDSHIRE

N., J. G. 'A summary catalogue of monumental art, existing in parish churches: Bedfordshire', T.G., 1, 1846, p.63-82 & 154-60. See also p.175.

BUCKINGHAMSHIRE

'Monumental inscriptions in the church of Wyrardisbury, lr Wraysbury, Co. Bucks., and a pedigree of Hassel of that place', C.T.G., 8, 1843, p.400-5. [Hassel pedigree 18-19th c.]

CAMBRIDGESHIRE

L., C. E. 'Extracts relating to the church of Horseheath, Co. Cambridge, from Cole's Mss. in the British Museum', C.T.G., 4, 1837, p.33-53. [Includes monumental inscriptions, list of rectors, and parish register extracts]

DERBYSHIRE

M., F. 'Derbyshire church notes', C.T.G., 1, 1834, p.34-51. [Notes on monumental inscriptions and heraldry at Staveley and Crich]

ESSEX

S., G. S. 'Epitaphs, and extracts from the register, at Stanway church, Essex', C.T.G., 4, 1837, p.305-8.

HAMPSHIRE

L., C. E. 'Church notes in the Hundred of Crondall, Hampshire', C.T.G., 7, 1841, p.211-42. [Includes monumental inscriptions]

L., C. E. ed. 'Church notes for Hampshire', C.T.G., 8, 1843, p.43-66, 132-9, 210-36, 369-400. [Includes monumental inscriptions for Bentley, Binsted, Dogmersfield, Elvetham, Eversley, South Warnborough, Froyle, Winchfield, Odiham, Basing, Cliddesden, Farley, Wallop, and Sherburne St. John]

L., C. E. 'Church notes of Hampshire', T.G., 2, 1853, p.306-11. [Notes on monumental inscriptions at Fyfield and Thruxton]

L., C. E. 'Church notes of Highclere and Burghclere, Co. Hants', T.G., 3, 1858, p.400-11. [Includes monumental inscriptions, Parish register abstracts, etc]

HUNTINGDONSHIRE

'Huntingdonshire church notes', T.G., 1, 1846, p.113-9. [Monumental inscriptions: Brampton, Catworth Magna and Chesterton]

KENT

'Church notes by Nicholas Charles, Lancaster Herald, temp James I - Greenwich - Fulham', T.G., 1, 1846, p.58-62. [Heraldry]

LONDON

N., J. G. 'Heraldic church notes and epitaphs taken at various periods in the church of St. Dunstan's in the West, Fleet-Street; to which are added extracts from the parish register', C.T.G., 4, 1837, p.96-127.

N., J. G. 'Register of the sepulchral inscriptions existing temp Hen. VIII in the church of the Grey Friars, London', C.T.G., 5, 1838, p.274-90 & 385-98.

See also under Kent

NORFOLK

M., G. 'Notes on Narburgh church, Norfolk', T.G., 2, 1853, p.224-33. [Monumental inscriptions]

NOTTINGHAMSHIRE

C., G. T. 'Church notes at Kingston upon Soar, Co. Notts, January 1842', C.T.G., 8, 1843, p.264-73.

SHROPSHIRE

P., H. 'Church notes from Ellesmere, Co. Salop', C.T.G., 3, 1836, p.89-94. [Includes monumental inscriptions]

SUFFOLK

Y., D. A. 'A summary catalogue of sepulchral memorials and remains of ancient art existing in parish churches:

Hundred of Blackbourn, Suffolk,	T.G., 1, 1846, p.280-93.
Hundred of Blything, Suffolk	T.G., 1, 1846, p.474-91.
Babergh Hundred, Suffolk	T.G., 1, 1846, p.161-75.
Hundred[s] of Bosmere and Claydon, Suffolk [and Carlford]	T.G., 1, 1846, p.538-56.
Hundreds of Colnies, Cosford &	T.G., 2, 1853, p.153-68.
Hundred of Hoxne	T.G., 2, 1853, p.234-46.
Town of Ipswich	T.G., 2, 1853, p.289-304.
Lackford Hundred	T.G., 2, 1853, p.385-97.
Hundred of Loes	T.G., 2, 1853, p.494-505.

'Heraldic notes taken at Clare, Co. Suffolk, in the reign of Queen Elizabeth', T.G., 2, 1853, p.398-402.

SURREY

S., G. S. 'Epitaphs formerly in Croydon church; and further extracts from the parish register of Croydon', C.T.G., 5, 1838, p.40-44.

S., G. S. 'Epitaphs, pennons and arms, formerly in Carshalton church, Surrey', C.T.G., 3, 1836, p.327-9.

WILTSHIRE

W., J. 'Account of the church of Bedwyn Magna in Wiltshire, with a list of the vicars, and extracts from the parish registers; and others from Bedwyn Parva, Frosfield, and Easton', C.T.G., 5, 1838, p.20-40. [Includes monumental inscriptions]

IRELAND

D., P. W. 'An account of the present state of Youghal church, including memorials of the Boyles; the College and Sir Walter Ralegh's house', T.G., 2, 1853, p.193-209. [Includes monumental inscriptions]

3. WILLS, INQUISITIONS POST MORTEM, AND FUNERAL CERTIFICATES

A. WILLS ETC.

B., G. ed. 'Transcripts and abstracts of wills', C.T.G., 5, 1838, p.88-91. [Sir Thomas Cheney or Cheyne <Lincolnshire, Nottinghamshire & Northamptonshire>, 1512; Thomas Montague of Hemington, Northamptonshire, 1514; John Broughton, esq <Bedfordshire, Cambridgeshire, Essex, Buckinghamshire, Huntingdonshire and Northamptonshire>, 1517]

Ditto, C.T.G., 5, 1838, p.305. [Charles, Earl of Worcester, 1524; Francis Catesby of Whiston, esq., 1527 <Northamptonshire>; George Kirkham, esq., 1527-8 <various counties>; Sir Walter Mauntell, 1523 <Northamptonshire>; Nicholas Woodhull, 1531 <various counties>]

Ditto, C.T.G., 6, 1840, p.98-101. [Charles Howard, Earl of Nottingham, 1587; Roger, Lord North, 1600]

Ditto, C.T.G., 7, 1841, p.42-7. [Anthony Wodhull, esq., 1538-9 <various counties>; Sir Robert Kirkham, 1657, <Northamptonshire>; John Butler, esq., 1557 <Northamptonshire>]

O., G. 'Wills of the families of Denys, Chamond and Arundell, from the episcopal register at Exeter', C.T.G., 4, 1837, p.169-77. [Wills of Richard Denys, rector of Powderham, 1532; Sir Thomas Denys, 1558; Dame Jane Chamond, 1550-1; Thomas Arundell of Talferne, esq., 1598]

S., G. S. 'Abstracts of ancient wills', C.T.G., 3, 1836, p.99-106. [Medieval; from Lansdowne Ms 860A: John Pavely, jnr., of Dover, 1300; John Merton, 1383; Robert Rouse Knt., 1383; Will Strete, 1383; John Devereux, Knt., 1383; Richard Fodringas of Risinge, Norfolk 1390., John Filliol of Essex, 1390., William Harpele, esq., 1392., John Waltham Bishop of Salisbury, 1395., Robert Bardolph of Maplederham Gurney, Oxfordshire 1395; Almarick de St. Amand, 1400; Eudo Hareleston of Essex and Cambridgeshire, 1400; William Dangle, Knt., 1401., Anne Lady Latimer, 1402., John Rodeney, arm, 1417; Thomas Fermbaud, arm., of Bladesden, 1419; Agnes Rodeney of Wiblecastle, 1420; Sir Will Cheney, 1442; John Point of North Wekendon, 1446; John Poynte esq. of North Wokenden, {i.e. North Ockenden, Essex?} 1469; Philip Thornbury, Knt. of Bigraue, Hertfordshire, 1452; William Brokas, senior, arm., 1454; Dame Elizabeth Frowick of Middlesex, 1455; Nicholas Carew, senior, of Bedyngton, Surrey, 1456; Edmund Inglethorpe, miles, 1456; Richard Hatfield of Steeple Morden, Cambridgeshire, 1467; Foulk Eytone. arm., {no date}; Andrew Ogard, Knt. {no date}; Richard Child of Harlton, Cambridgeshire, 1488; John Shardlowe, Knt., 1484; Elizabeth Lady Say of Erbury, Warwickshire, 1464.]

SURTEES, Robert, ed.] 'Wills of the families of Scrope, Salvayn, Bowes, De La Pole, Fulthorpe and Dautre', C.T.G., 2, 1835, p.148-51. [Yorkshire; 15th c.]

Bonville

D., J. 'Documents relating to the estate of Sir William Bonville of Shute, Co. Devon, temp Edw. III', C.T.G., 8, 1843, p.237-47. [Includes will, 1407, and deeds]

Hungerford

B., G. 'Abstracts of Hungerford wills', C.T.G., 7, 1841, p.70-2. [Hungerford family; 15-16th c.]

Mautravers

B., T. ' Will of Sir John Mautravers, Knt., 1386', C.T.G., 4, 1837, p.179-80.

Mekilfelde

B., W. H. 'The will of William Mekilfelde, esq., of Henham, Co. Suffolk', C.T.G., 5, 1838, p.12-18. [1439]

Robson

L., C. E. ed. 'Inventory of the goods &c of John Robson, Master of the College of Lingfield, Co. Surrey, in 1524', C.T.G., 8, 1843, p.39-42.

Say

A., G. J. 'Will of Sir William Say, Knt., 1529', T.G., 1, 1846, 412-21.

Stafford

G., B. W. 'Will of John Stafford of Marlwood, esq., 1596', T.G., 1, 1846, p.142-4. [Gloucestershire]

B. INQUISITIONS POST MORTEM

A., G. J. ed. 'Minutes from the inquisitions post mortem relating to Middlesex', T.G., 1, 1846, p.330-2 & 520-3.

M. 'Abstract of inquisitions post mortem, temp. Hen. III, for the counties of Somerset and Dorset', C.T.G., 2, 1835, p.48-56 & 168-74.

Berkrolls

'Inquisition on the death of Sir Laurence Berkrolls in 1411', T.G., 1, 1846, 533-5. [Inquisition post mortem]

Fitzpain

G., ed. 'Additional documents relating to the family of Fitzpain and the coheirs of Bryan', C.T.G., 3, 1836, p.398-400. [Inquisitions post mortem for Robert Baron Fitzpain, 1354; {Dorset}, and Sir John de St. Maur, 4 Hen. V {Somerset}]

Hawkeswell

P. 'Abbreviatio inquisitionis post mortem Joh'is de Hawkeswell, in Com. Northumberland, A 10 H. 5', C.T.G., 2, 1835, p.387.

St Maur

See Fitzpain

C. FUNERAL CERTIFICATES

N., J. G. 'Funeral certificates', C.T.G., 4, 1837, p.370-84.

N., J. G., 'Funeral certificates, temp Elizabeth', C.T.G. 3, 1836, p.286-94.

Baker

'Funeral certificate of Sir Richard Baker, of Sisinghurst, Kent, 1594', T.G., 2, 1853, p.383-4.

Knevett

L., C. E. 'Funeral certificate of Sir Henry Knevett and his lady', T.G., 1, 1846, p.469-73. [Wiltshire]

4. FAMILY HISTORIES AND GENEALOGIES

A. GENERAL

B., B. 'Dugdale's Mss. additions to his baronage', C.T.G., 1, 1834, p.51-9 & 209-26; 2, 1835, p.1-16, 179-224, & 329-64.

B., W. D. 'Genealogical additions to the history of Stockton upon Tees', T.G., 2, 1853, p.73-88, 97-123. See also p.550-9.

M. 'Extracts from the chronicles or cartulary of the Abbey of Meaux, Co. York, containing the genealogies of Scurres, Hyldehard and Stutevyll', C.T.G., 1, 1834, p.9-13. [Includes list of benefactors buried at Meaux]

Y., C. G. 'Additions to Dugdale's Baronage, from the Ms. collections of Francis Townsend, esq., Windsor Herald', C.T.G., 4, 1836, p.351-70; 5, 1838, p.1-11, 141-57, & 312-28; 6, 1840, p.68-89, 147-57, 245-65, & 392-9; 7, 1841, p.47-69, 129-61, 249-72 & 378-93; 8, 1843, p. 67-80 & 155-88.

'Pedigrees from the plea-rolls, &c', C.T.G., 1, 1834, p.128-48 & 254-76.

N., N. H., 'Pedigrees showing the relationship between many of the nobility and gentry and the blood royal, compiled about the year 1505', C.T.G., 1, 1834, p.295-319.

B. PARTICULAR FAMILIES

ALFORD

F., C. 'Pedigree of Alford, of Meaux Abbey, Yorkshire', C.T.G., 4, 1837, p.177-8. [16-17th c.]

ANNESLEY

See De La Pole

ARDEN

'On the connection of Arderne, or Arden, of Cheshire, with the Ardens of Warwickshire', T..G., 1, 1846, p.208-15. [Includes pedigree]

ARUNDELL

O., G. 'Arundelliana', C.T.G., 3, 1836, p.389-95. [Cornwall; medieval. Includes the will of Sir John Arundell, 1433]

G., B. W. 'Further particulars respecting Sir Edward Arundel, Knt., and the manor of Aynho, Co. Northampton', T.G., 3, 1858, p.240-55.

N., N. H. 'Genealogical statement respecting Beatrix, wife of Thomas, Earl of Arundel, and Beatrix, wife of of Sir Gilbert Talbot', C.T.G., 1, 1834, p.80-90. [Includes pedigrees, 13-15th c.]

See also Honywood

ASHBY

G., H. ''Genealogical notices of the family of Ashby of Harefield, in the county of Middlesex', C.T.G., 5, 1838, p.125-41. [Includes pedigree, 17-19th c.]

BABINGTON

C., G. T. 'Inedited additions to the pedigree of Babington', T.G., 1, 1846, p.133-41, 259-79 & 333-43. See also p.396. [Nottinghamshire Oxfordshire, Northumberland, & Staffordshire]

'The pedigree of the family of Babington of Dethick and Kingston, with their alliances, chiefly in the counties of Stafford, Nottingham and Derby', C.T.G., 8, 1843, p.313-60. [13-19th c.]

BAGOT

See Stafford

BARD

S., G. S. 'Pedigree of Bard of Lincolnshire, Middlesex and Bucks., and Viscount Bellamont of the Kingdom of Ireland', C.T.G., 4, 1837, p.59-61. [16-18th c.]

BARTON

HODGSON, John. 'Entail in the family of Barton of Fryton, of property in Havergate, York', C.T.G., 2, 1835, p.67-8. [14th c. deed]

BEDFORD

See Edwards

BEKE

BEKE, Charles T. 'Observations on the pedigree of the family of Beke of Edresby, in the county of Lincoln', C.T.G., 4, 1837, p.331-45. [13-14th c.]

'Some particulars relative to Colonel Richard Beke of Hadenham, in the county of Buckingham, and to a pardon under the Great Seal, granted to him XII Car. II, in a letter to John Lee, esq., Ll. D., F. R. S., &c., from Charles T. Beke, esq., Ph. D., F.S.A', T.G., 3, 1858, p.155-77. [Includes deed abstracts, 17th c., & pedigree, 15-18th c.]

BISHOP

E., W. S. 'Pedigrees of Bishop', T.G., 3, 1858, p.361-70. [Various counties; c.15-18th c.]

BOKELAND

See Polhill

BOTELER

See Stanley

BOTFIELD

See Thynne

BOTREAX

See Stafford

BROOKE

See Cobham

BRYAN

G. 'Documents relative to the families of Bryan, Fitzpain, Ponynges, and others, the coheirs of Sir Guy Bryan, K. G.' C.T.G., 3, 1836, p.250-78. [Various counties; 14-16th c.]

BURTON

READER, W. 'The Burtons of Carsley, near Coventry', T.G., 1, 1846, p.579-80. [Letter to the editor]

Z., X. Y. 'The Burtons of Coventry', T.G., 1, 1846, 493-5. [Letter to the editor]

CAREW

'Particulars relative to a branch of the family of Carew, seated in the county of Cork', C.T.G., 5, 1838, p.93-99. [14-18th c.]

CHAMBERLAYNE

G., H. 'Account of the several branches of the family of Chamberlayne', C.T.G., 3, 1836, p.95-8. [Medieval]

CHANDOS

See De La Pole

CHESLYN

'Epitaph commemorative of the family of Cheslyn, at Diseworth church, Leicestershire', C.T.G., 3, 1836, p.314-5. [17-18th c.]

CLARKE

See D'Oyly

CLERKE

See D'Oyly

CLINTON

See Meignell

CLOSE

B., W. D. 'The Close family of Richmond, Yorkshire', T.G., 1, 1846, p.557-61.

COBHAM

N., J. G. 'Memorials of the family of Cobham', C.T.G., 7, 1841, p.320-54. [Medieval; also includes notes on Brooke and De La Pole families, also includes deeds]

COCKAYNE

ADAMS, G. E. 'Some account of the family of Cockayne, Lords Viscount Cullen, and of the parish of Rushton, Co. Northampton, their principal residence', T.G., 3, 1858, p.437-61.

COKE

B., J. 'Sir Edward Coke's Vade mecum', C.T.G., 6, 1840, p.108-22. [Autobiographical notes by Coke]

COLLIER

See Dodington

COURTHOPE

'Ancient deeds in illustration of the descent of the Courthopes, of Goudhurst, Co. Kent, and Wyleigh, Co. Sussex', C.T.G., 2, 1835, p.393-8.

DABRIDGECOURT

L., C. E. 'Pedigree of Dabridgecourt, of Stratfield Say, Co. Hants', T.G., 1, 1846, p.197-207.

DAKYS

See De La Pole

DE BOKELAND

See Polhill

DE LA POLE

Z., X. Y. 'Notices of the family of Pole or De La Pole, of Derbyshire, and of other families connected with it', T.G., 1, 1846, p.176-9. [Includes pedigree, 15-16th c; also Dakys, Chandos, and Annesley]

See also Cobham

DEIVELL

See Ellis

DIZNEY

See Ellis

DODINGTON

'The families of Dodington and Collier', T.G., 3, 1858, p.568-75. [Dodington of Somerset; Collier of Staffordshire]

D'OYLY

B., W. D. 'Addition to the D'Oyly pedigree', T.G., 1, 1846, p.567.

B., W. D. 'Genealogy physiologically considered, with a "tail female" pedigree of D'Oyly, by Marston, by Kirby, by Kynnersley, by Clarke, by Clerke, by Holman', T.G., 2, 1853, p.1-27.

B., W. D. 'Pedigree of the early D'Oylys', T.G., 1, 1846, p.366-78. See also p.396. [Medieval; various counties]

DREW

'Genealogy of the family of Drew', T.G., 2, 1853, p.209-15. [Devon, Kerry, Waterford and Limerick; Pedigree, medieval-19th c.]

EDWARDS

E., W. S. 'Pedigree of the family of Edwards of Henlow, Arlsey, Clifton and Little Barford, Bedfordshire; with their descent in the families of Bedford, Rainsford, Rowe, Merriden, Windrest and Wye', C.T.G., 6, 1840, p.290-3. [15-19th c.]

ELDRED

S., G. S. 'Genealogical notes of the Eldred family', C.T.G., 6, 1840, p.295-7. [Essex and London; 17-18th c.]

ELLIS

E., W. S. 'Pedigree of Ellis and Fitz-Ellis', T.G., 3, 1858, p.270-97.

E., W. S. 'Remarks on the arms assigned to the name of Ellis and its synonyms, tending to show a common origin of most of the families bearing them, and of Lacy, Lucy, St. Leger, Lizures, St. Liz, Dizney, Deivell, Holles, &c', T.G., 3, 1858, p.385-99.

FITZ-AILWARD

See Stanley

FITZ-ELLIS

See Ellis

FITZHERBERT

See Meignell

FITZPAIN

See Bryan

FOLJAMBE

JOHNSTONE, Nathaniel. 'Notices of the family of Foljambe during the reigns of King Henry III and King Edward I, chiefly from the private charters of the family', C.T.G., 1, 1834, p.91-111 & 333-61. [of Tideswell and Wormhill, Derbyshire]

JOHNSTONE, Nathaniel. 'History of the family of Foljambe', C.T.G., 2, 1835, p.68-90. [16-18th c. Continuation of previous article]

FRANCEIS

See Meignell

FRECHEVILLE

HUNTER, Joseph. 'Additions to the pedigree of the Freschvile family, and a few corrections', C.T.G., 4, 1837, p.384-8.

M., F. 'Pedigree of the Frecheville and Musard families, lords of Crich and Staveley in Derbyshire', C.T.G., 4, 1837, p.1-28 & 181-218.

FREMINGHAM

P., B. 'De Fremingham, Isley and Pimpe', T.G., 1, 1846, p.514-9. [Kent; Includes pedigree, 14-16th c., & deeds]

FULHAM

BRAY, W. 'Pedigree of the family of Fulham, of Compton, Surrey', C.T.G., 1, 1834, p.17-19. [17-18th c.]

GILL

See Gyll

GIRLINGTON

R., J. 'Pedigree of Girlington, of Girlington Hall, in the parish of Wycliffe, in Richmondshire, and North Riding of the county of York', C.T.G., 6, 1840, p.190-1. [13-17th c.]

GODFREY

'The domestic chronicle of Thomas Godfrey, esq', T.G., 2, 1853, p.450-67.

GORHAMBURY

G., G. C. 'On the descent of the manor of Gorhambury in Hertfordshire, and of the Anglo-British family from whom that estate derived its name', C.T.G., 5, 1838, p.182-99 & 329-45. [Includes pedigrees 12-15th c., including that of Gorhambury families of Leicestershire and Northamptonshire]

G., C. G. 'Some additional particulars and charters relating to the Anglo-Breton family De Gorram', C.T.G., 6, 1840, p.284-9; 8, 1843, p.81-116. [Hertfordshire and Northamptonshire]

GOSPATRICK

HODGSON, John. 'Charters respecting the Gospatrick and other northern families, from the Newminster chartulary and Lord Wallace's muniments', C.T.G., 3, 1836, p.396-8.

GRESHAM

'Births of the children of Sir John Gresham, Lord mayor of London in 1547, by his first wife Mary, daughter and co-heir of Thomas Ipswell', T.G., 2, 1853, p.512-4.

GREYSTOCK

N., J. G., ed. 'Pedigrees by Sir Thomas Wriothesley, Garter', C.T.G., 2, 1835, p.160-2. [Greystock, 15th c; Strangways, medieval]

GYLLE

G., G. 'The genealogy of the family of Gylle, or Gill, of Hertfordshire, illustratred by wills and other documents', C.T.G., 8, 1843, p.274-97. [Pedigrees, 15-19th c.]

'Emendations and addenda to the Gyll pedigree in the eighth volume of Collectanea Topog. et Geneal', T.G., 2, 1853, p.560-4.

HALES

READER, W. 'Documents relating to the family of Hales, of Coventry, and the foundation of the Free School', T.G., 1, 1846, p.120-32.

HAMPTON

E., W. S. 'Pedigree of Hampton of Surrey and Sussex', C.T.G., 6, 1840, p.294.

HARLAKENDEN

STEINMAN, G. Steinman. 'Pedigree of Harlakenden of Kent and Essex', T.G., 1, 1846, p.228-58. [13-18th c.] See also p.395-6.

STEINMAN, G. Steinman. 'Deeds of the family of Harlakenden', T.G., 2, 1853, p.215-23. [Letter to the editor; Essex deeds, 17th c.]

HERBERT

Y., C. G. 'The Earldom of Glamorgan: addendum for Dugdale', C.T.G., 7, 1841, p190-6. [Monmouthshire; Pedigree, 17-19th c.]

HERIZ

See Smith

HERON

S., G. S. 'Pedigree of Heron, of Addiscombe, Surrey', C.T.G., 2, 1835, p.166-7.

HIDE

See Urmeston

HODILOW

B., W. D. 'An account of the family of Hodilow, of Cambridgeshire, Essex, Northamptonshire, and Middlesex', T.G., 2, 1853, p.28-72. [15-17th c.]

HODY

'Notices of the family of Hody, &c', C.T.G., 6, 1840, p.22-31. [Includes wills of Sir John Hody of Pillesdon, Dorset, 1441, & John Jewe, 1416 <Dorset>]

HOLLES

See Ellis

HOLMAN

See D'Oyly

HONING

'Description of a picture of the family of Honing, temp Eliz., with their pedigree', C.T.G., 7, 1841, p.394-400. [Suffolk]

HONYWOOD

BAYLEY, W. D'Oyly. 'The relationship of the Honywoods, Baronets, of Kent to Mr. Frazer Honywood the banker', T.G., 2, 1853, p.189-91. [Letter to the editor; includes pedigree, 17-18th c.]

'Honywood evidences', T.G., 1, 1846, p.568-76; 2, 1853, p.169-85, 256-69 & 312-39; 2, 1853, p.433-46. [Includes medieval pedigree & deeds, etc, to 17th c; also notices of Sir Edward Arundel of Aynho, Northamptonshire, 15th c., with a pedigree of his descendants]

'The posterity of Mary Honywood at her death in 1620', T.G., 1, 1846, 397-411. [Various counties]

HORD

E., W. S. 'Pedigree of the family of Hord, of Salop, Oxon, and Surrey', T.G., 1, 1846, p.33-42.

HORNE

S., G. S. 'Pedigree of De Horne of Essex', C.T.G., 2, 1835, p.286-8. [16-19th c.]

HURLY

D'ALTON, John. 'Notes on the Cathedral of Emly, and the family of Hurly', T.G., 3, 1858, p.462-7. [Tipperary]

HUSTLER

B., W. D. 'Hustler of Acklam in Cleveland', T.G., 1, 1846, 497-9.

INGRAM

S., E. P. 'Notices of the family of Ingram, of Little Wolford, in the county of Warwickshire', C.T.G., 8, 1843, p. 140-6.

IPSWELL

See Gresham

ISLEY

See Fremingham

KIRBY

See D'Oyly

KYNNERSLEY

See D'Oyly

LACY

See Ellis

LATHOM

See Stanley

LIZURES

See Ellis

LOVETT

S., E. P. 'Deeds relating to the family of Lovett of Northamptonshire, from originals in the possession of the Earl Ferrers', C.T.G., 6, 1840, p.299-300.

LUCY

See Ellis

LUNSFORD

N., J. G. 'Pedigree of the family of Lunsford, of Lunsford and Wilegh, Co. Sussex', C.T.G., 4, 1837, p.139-56.

MALTRAVERS

S., G. S. 'Pedigree of Maltravers, Baron Maltravers', C.T.G., 3, 1836, p.77-9. [Dorset; medieval]

S., G. S. 'Pedigree of Mautravers, of Litchet and of Crowell and Hook', C.T.G., 6, 1840, p.334-61. [Dorset; 11-15th c; includes deeds]

MARCHE

B., W. D. 'Pedigree of Marche of the Isle of Ely', T.G., 2, 1853, p.246-53.

MARSTON

See D'Oyly

MAUNSELL

B., G. 'Poetical history of the family of Maunsell', C.T.G., 1, 1834, p.389-94.

MAUTRAVERS

See Maltravers

MEIGNELL

Z., X. Y. ''On the descent of Meignell and Clinton', T.G., 1, 1846, p.349-65. See also 492-3. [Derbyshire; Medieval pedigrees of Meignell, Clinton, Franceis or Roeman, & Fitzherbert]

MERRIDEN

See Edwards

MORGAN

L., C. E. 'Sir Thomas Morgan, Knt', T.G., 1, 1846, p.496.

MORTON

S., G. S. Pedigree of Morton of Whitehorse, in the parish of Croydon, Surrey', C.T.G., 3, 1836, p.169-71.

MUSARD

See Frecheville

NICHOLL

NICHOLS, F. M. 'An account of the family of Nicholl, Nicholls, or Nicolls of London, and of Ampthill, Co. Bedford, with notes of their wills', T.G., 3, 1858, p.533-44. [Pedigree, 16-17th c.]

NORRES

'Genealogical declaration respecting the family of Norres, written by Sir William Norres of Speke, Co. Lancaster, in the year 1563, accompanied by an abstract of ancient charters', T.G., 2, 1853, p.357-83.

OGLE

S., T. 'Pedigree of Ogle, of Pinchbeck, Co. Lincoln', C.T.G., 6, 1840, p.194-6. [16th c.]

PARR

P., H. 'Early pedigrees of the Parr family', T.G., 3, 1858, p.352-60. [Westmorland, Lancashire & Cheshire; pedigree, 14-16th c.] See also additions and corrigenda, p.597-8.

PERCY

T., J. F. 'Documents relating to the Percy family', C.T.G., 6, 1840, p.370-80. [Deeds, 16th c; will of Kateryna, Countess of Northumberland, 1542]

Y., C. G. 'Claim of James Percy, the trunk-maker, to the Earldom of Northumberland, as descended from Sir Ingelram or Ingram Percy; will of Sir Ingram; descent and succession of the Percys of Northumberland', C.T.G., 6, 1840, p.266-83. [Pedigree 14-17th c; will, 1538]

'Younger branches of the house of Percy', C.T.G., 2, 1835, p.57-66. [Includes pedigree, various counties, 15-18th c., together with wills of Henry Percy, Earl of Northumberland, 1485, Josselyn Percy of Newland, 1532, George Percy, rector of Rothbury, Northumberland, and Caldbeck, Cumberland, 1474, and Robert Percy of Terington, Yorkshire, 1544]

PIMPE

See Fremingham

PITCHFORD

See Pycheford

PLOMER

BRUCE, William Downing. 'Pedigree of the family of Plomer', T.G., 2, 1853, p.278-80. [Hertfordshire; 17-19th c.]

POLHILL

Z., X. Y. 'The Polhill, or Polley, and De Bokeland families, deduced from the visitation of Kent in 1619, by Philpot, and of 1633, from Hasted and Harris' histories of Kent, Berry's Kentish pedigrees, and Add. ms. 5711, &c', T.G., 1, 1846, p.180-93.

'Registries of the family of Polhill', T.G., 1, 1846, p.577-9.

PONYNGES

See Bryan

PYCHEFORD

B., W. D. 'Pedigree of Pycheford', T.G., 2, 1853, p.506-11. [or Pitchford. Shropshire; pedigree, 12-17th c.]

RAINSFORD

See Edwards

ROEMAN

See Meignell

ROOKWOOD

'Vetustissima prosapia Rookewodorum de Stanningefilde in Comitatu Suffolciae', C.T.G., 2, 1835, p.120-47. [Rookwood family. Includes pedigrees, 14-19th c.]

ROWE

See Edwards

SACKVILLE

N., J. G. 'Sepulchral memorials of the Sackville family, at Withyam, Sussex', C.T.G., 3, 1836, p.295-306. [15-18th c; includes extracts from parish register]

ST. LEGER

See Ellis

ST. LIZ

See Ellis

SCUDAMORE

G., H. 'Sepulchral memorials of the Scudamore family at Home-Lacy, Co. Hereford', C.T.G., 4, 1837, p.256-9. [16-18th c.]

SHEFFIELD

C., S. H. 'Extracts from the parish register of Seton, Co. Rutland, relative to the family of Sheffield', C.T.G., 1, 1834, p.171-3. [16-17th c.]

C., S. H. 'Pedigree of Sheffield of Seton, Co. Rutland, and Navestock, Co. Essex', C.T.G., 4, 1837, p.259-60. [17-18th c.]

SMITH

'Grant of arms in 1499, and of a crest in 1565, to the family of Smith, alias Heriz, of the county of Leicester', T.G., 3, 1858, p.255-60.

STAFFORD

M., F. 'Marriage contract of Sir John Stafford and Anne daughter of William Lord Botreaux, 1426', C.T.G., 4, 1837, p.249-55. [Somerset and Dorset]

P. 'Origin of the family of Stafford', C.T.G., 1, 1834, p.249. [Charter of William de Stafford, son of Hervei Bagot, to the Priory of St. Thomas, Stafford; grant of Villa de Drayton]

STANLEGH

S., T. 'Deed relating to the family of Stanlegh, of Stanlegh, Co. Derby', C.T.G., 2, 1835, p.56-7.

STANLEY

O., Geo. 'On the Stanley legend and the houses of Boteler, Fitz-Ailward, Lathom and Stanley', C.T.G., 6, 1840, p.1-21. [Lancashire; c.11-17th c.]

STRANGWAYS

See Greystock

STUMPE

J., J. G. 'Memorials of the family of Stumpe of Malmesbury', C.T.G., 7, 1841, p.81-4. [Wiltshire; pedigree, 16-17th c.]

TALBOT

See Arundel

THYNNE

MORRIS, Joseph. 'The family of Thynne, otherwise Botfield', T.G., 3, 1858, p.468-91. [Shropshire; pedigree, 15-19th c.]

TREGOZE

B., W. D. 'Pedigree of the Tregoze family', T.G., 2, 1853, p.126-36. [Various counties; 12-14th c.]

TURNER

B., W. D. 'Turner family of Kirkleatham, North Riding of Yorkshire', T.G., 1, 1846, p.505-9.

UFFORD

S., G. S. 'Pedigree of Ufford', T.G., 2, 1853, p.271-7. [Suffolk; 13-15th c.]

'Difficulties in the pedigree of Ufford - the Bowet', T.G., 1, 1846, p.299-300. [Correspondence by F.C.A.S. & D.A.Y.]

UNDERHILL

S., E. P. 'Some account of the family of Underhill', C.T.G., 6, 1840, p.380-4. [Warwickshire and Staffordshire; 16-18th c.]

URMESTONE

O., Geo. 'A genealogical certificate, compiled temp Henry VI, as to the descent of the lordship of Urmestone, Co. Lancaster, from the grantee of Adam de Urmeston to the Hides', C.T.G., 8, 1843, p. 146-52. [Includes medieval pedigrees of Urmeston and Hide]

WALEROND

L., C. E. 'Seal of Isabella Walerond', T.G., 1, 1846, p.28-32. [Includes pedigree of Walerond, 12-14th c.]

WICKHAM

L., C. E. 'Descent of the family of Wickham of Swalcliffe, Co. Oxon, and their kindred to the founder of New College', C.T.G., 2, 1835, p.225-45 & 368-87; 3, 1836, p.178-239 & 345-76. [Medieval-19th c; includes pedigree]

MARTIN, Charles Wykeham. 'Was William of Wykeham of the family of Swalcliffe?', T.G., 3, 1858, p.49-76. [Includes pedigree, 11-18th c.]

WINDREST

See Edwards

WYE

See Edwards

YATE

N., J. 'Pedigree of the 'Yates of Cheshire' and therein of Dr. Thomas Yate, Principal of Brasenose College, Oxford', T.G., 1, 1846, 421-31.

5. HERALDRY

G., S. 'Copy of a roll of arms (of the reign of Edw. III) in the possession of Stacey Grimaldi, esq', C.T.G., 2, 1835, p.320-8.

L., C. E. 'Roll of the arms of the knights at the tournament at Dunstable, in 7 Edw. III', C.T.G., 4, 1837, p.389-95.

L., C. E. 'Tournament at Stepney, 2 Edw. II', C.T.G., 4, 1837, p.61-72. [Roll of arms]

S., G. S. 'Some account of the arms and other paintings, now or formerly in the windows of the church of St. Giles, Camberwell', C.T.G., 2, 1835, p.114-9.

W., T. 'Banners, standards and badges, temp Hen. VIII', C.T.G., 3, 1836, p.49-76.

W., T. 'Description of the stained glass in Charlecote House near Stratford on Avon, the seat of George Lucy, esquire', C.T.G., 4, 1837, p.346-50. [Heraldic]

Y., C. J. 'Arms in the Great Chamber at the Charterhouse', C.T.G., 2, 1835, p.91-3.

6. RECORDS OF NATIONAL AND LOCAL ADMINISTRATION

FERGUSON, James F. 'Account of Sir Toby Caulfield rendered to the Irish Exchequer, relating to the chattel property of the Earl of Tyrone and other fugitives from Ulster in the year 1616', T.G., 3, 1858, p.77-94.

FERGUSON, James F. 'Contest between the king's Purveyors and the secular clergy of Meath, in the 3 Edw. II', T.G., 3, 1858, p.223-39.

G., H. 'Grant of the wardship of Marmaduke Thwenge, 1588', C.T.G., 3, 1836, p.172-3.

DEVON

T., ed. 'Charter of John King of Castille and Leon, Duke of Lancaster, dated 1386, appointing Edward Earl of Devonshire his Lieutenant in that county, from the original in the possession of Sir John Trevelyan, Bart., of Nettlecombe, Co. Somerset', C.T.G., 2, 1835, p.319.

HAMPSHIRE

M., F. 'Taxation of the tenth and fifteenth in Hampshire in 1334', C.T.G., 1, 1834, p.175-83. [List of payments by hundred and parish; no personal names]

NORTHUMBERLAND

See also under Yorkshire

SHROPSHIRE

M., G. 'Forests of Shropshire', C.T.G., 3, 1836, p.111-21. [Perambulation, 1300]

M., G. 'Ottleiana, or, letters &c relating to Shropshire, written during and subsequent to the Civil War, chiefly addressed to Sir Francis Ottley and forming part of the Ottley mss', C.T.G., 5, 1838, p.291-304; 6, 1840, p.21-37; 7, 1841, p.84-110 & p.303-19.

SUSSEX

C., W., ed. 'Muster roll for the Rape of Hastings, 13 Edw. III', C.T.G., 7, 1841, p.118-28.

YORKSHIRE

N., J. G. 'Charges made by Christopher Lascelles, gent., against Sir Robert Riche, Chancellor of the Court of Augmentations, for malversation in granting leases of church lands in Yorkshire and Northumberland', T.G., 2, 1853, p.285-7.

'Subsidy roll of the Wapentake of Staincross, in the West Riding of Yorkshire, in 1663', C.T.G., 3, 1836, p.333-8.

7. PRIVATE ESTATES

P., R. B. 'Documents respecting Matilda, Countess of Chester, and Hugh surnamed Kevelioc, her son, Earl of Chester', C.T.G., 2, 1835, p.247-9. [Includes 12-13th c. pedigree of Earls of Chester; precept re the Hundred of Repton, and mandate concerning rents in Oldney, Buckinghamshire, and Tadwell, Lincolnshire]

T., W. C. 'Charter of Robert last Earl of Mellent to his grand-daughter Mary and her husband Peter de Pratellis, dated in 1201', C.T.G., 2, 1835, p.390.

T., W. C. 'Two deeds of Simon Ralegh, regarding his property in Wales, from the originals in vellum, in the possession of Sir John Trevelyan, Bart', C.T.G., 2, 1835, p.391-2. [Medieval]

'Charter relating to Leysanteston, 32 Edw. I, 1304', T.G., 2, 1853, p.186. [Perhaps in South Wales]

'Survey, temp Phil. & Mar., of various estates late belonging to the Earl of Devon', T.G., 1, 1846, p.43-58; p.145-53 p.223-8; p.343-8 [Estates in Somerset, Dorset, Devon, Cornwall, Wiltshire & Staffordshire]

BUCKINGHAMSHIRE

BAYLEY, W. D'Oyly. 'Ancient deeds, Bucks and Oxon', T.G., 2, 1853, p.340-44. [Fawley & Hambledon, Buckinghamshire; Chislehampton and Chibenhurst, Oxfordshire]

CAMBRIDGESHIRE

L., L. B. 'Early charters relating to land in Babraham, Cambridgeshire', C.T.G., 4, 1837, p.137-8.

'Extracts from a private chartulary, written chiefly by Talbot Pepys, of Impington, Co. Cambridge, esq.', T.G., 3, 1858, p.97-109. [16-17th c; includes will of John Pepys of Cottenham, Cambridgeshire, 1589]

CO. CORK

CAULFIELD, Richard. 'Chartae Tyrryanae', T.G., 3, 1858, p.110-22. [Tyrry family deeds relating to Cork, etc, 15-16th c.]

DEVON

N., J. G. 'Devonshire charters connected with the family of Ferrers', C.T.G., 8, 1843, p.33-5. [Medieval]

ESSEX

N., J. G. 'Indenture relative to the family of Maxey and to various lands in Essex', C.T.G., 2, 1835, p.245-6. [16th c.]

'Charter of King Henry II, granting the vill of Reines, now Rayne, in Essex, to Gervase de Wellis', T.G., 3, 1858, p.512.

Y., C. G. 'Notices of Sir Richard Arundell; grant and release of the manor of Markedych in Essex; lands called Eyres, Baldwynes, and Bretons; lands in the Liberty of Havering; will of Sir Richard Arundell, and the pedigree of his line of the Fitzalan family', C.T.G., 6, 1840, p.1-20. [Fitzalan pedigree, 14-16th c; will dated 1418]

GLAMORGANSHIRE

F., G. G. 'Charter of Gilbert de Turberville relating to the manor of Landimore in Gower, 9 Edw. III, 1335', T.G., 2, 1853, p.269-71.

FRANCIS, G. G. 'Lease of all the coals in the Lordships of Gower and Kilvey, from the Earl of Worcester to Sir Mathyas Cradock, Knt., A.D. 1526', T.G., 1, 1846, p.565-6.

F., G. G. 'Letters of quittance from Sir Rhys ap Thomas, K.G., to the tenants of Edward Stradling, esq., A. D. 1494', T.G., 1, 1846, 562-4.

T., J. M. 'Deeds connected with Newcastle and Swansea, Glamorganshire, in the possession of C. R. Mansel Talbot', C.T.G., 8, 1843, p.36-7. [13-14th c.]

'Charter relating to lands in the lordship of Gower and entail in the family of Penrice, 2 Edw. III', T.G., 1, 1846, p.536-7.

'Deed relating to an estate in the lordship of Kilvey, Co. Glamorgan, 4 Edw. II, 1311', T.G., 2, 1853, p.185.

'Deed relating to Merthyr Mawr, Co. Glamorgan, in 2 Edw. III, 1328', T.G., 2, 1853, p.305.

HEREFORDSHIRE

S., G. S. 'Charter of Godfrey Giffard, Bishop of Worcester, 1258-1301, to his nephew Alexander de Fryvile, granting land at Mawene (now Marden) in Herefordshire', C.T.G., 4, 1837, p.248.

HUNTINGDONSHIRE

L., L. B. 'Charters relating to the manor of Hemington in the parish of Stilton, Huntingdonshire', C.T.G., 4, 1837, p.219-22. [14-15th c.]

L., L. B. 'Deeds relating to the manor of Stilton, Co. Huntingdon, and the families of Bell and Sanky', C.T.G., 4, 1837, p.133-7. [15th c.]

N., J. G. 'Attestation to the tenure of a pasture called Broghton Lesewe, near the park of Buckden, Co. Huntingdon, made in 5 Hen. VI', C.T.G., 8, 1843, p. 32-3.

LONDON AND MIDDLESEX

S., E. P. 'Lease of the moiety of Essex House in the Strand, London, anno 1639 (14 Charles I)', C.T.G., 8, 1843, p.309-12.

MONMOUTHSHIRE

'Charter of Walter Waleran conveying the manor of Mersfield, Co. Monmouth, to Payne de Turberville, circa 1200', T.G., 2, 1853, p.287-8.

NORTHAMPTONSHIRE

L., L. B. ''Exemplification of records and charters relating to the manor of Morton Pinkeny and other manors of the Barony of Pinkeney in the county of Northampton, temp Edw. II & III, &c', C.T.G., 4, 1837, p.223-31.

NOTTINGHAMSHIRE

B., W. H., 'Charter of Henry III granting the manor of Dunham in Nottinghamshire to Ralph Fitz-Nicholas, 4 May 1233', C.T.G., 1, 1834, p.173-4.

OXFORDSHIRE

G., H. 'The manor of Bampton, Co. Oxford, and family of Horde', T.G., 2, 1853, p.515-20. [Medieval deeds; notes on the 16-17th c. family]

See also Buckinghamshire

SHROPSHIRE

'Tenants in capite and sub-tenants in Shropshire, circ. temp. Edw I', C.T.G., 1, 1834, p.111-21.

SOMERSET

T., W. C. 'Charters relating to Nettlecombe, Co. Somerset, and the families of Mareschall (Earls of Pembroke) and of Ralegh', C.T.G., 2, 1835, p.163-6. [Medieval]

SUSSEX

C., W. 'Deeds relating to the manor of Wyleigh in Ticehurst, Co. Sussex, and to the family of Courthope, in the possession of George Courthope, of Wyleigh, esq', C.T.G., 2, 1835, p.279-85. [16th c.]

WESTMORLAND

'Chirograph between Lady Margaret de Ros and William de Stirkeland relative to certain customs on his lands in Westmereland, &c., 1281', T.G., 2, 1853, p.187-9.

WILTSHIRE

L., 'Grant of the manor of Corsham, in Wiltshire, to the tenants, as farmers in fee, by Richard, Earl of Cornwall', C.T.G., 2, 1835, p.317-8. [14th c.]

YORKSHIRE

BRUCE, Wm. Downing. 'Charter of Robert de Neville, of land at Bolleby, in the parish of Easington, Co. York', T.G., 1, 1846, p.513-4. [13th c. Letter to the editor]

B., W. D. 'Notices of Thimbleby and Ellerbeck, in the parish of Osmotherley, North Riding of Yorkshire, with pedigrees of Peirse, Walton, Hirst, and Bayley', T.G., 1, 1846, p.523-33.

D., R. 'Early charters relating to the manor of Kirkby-under-Knoll, in the North Riding of Yorkshire', T.G., 1, 1846, p.216-23.

JACKSON, Charles. 'Notes from deeds relating to estates at Wheatley, Bentley, &c, in the county of York, from a Ms book at Wheatley', T.G., 3, 1858, p.513-32.

8. CORPORATE ESTATES

B., W. H., 'Grant from the Corporation of London to the College of Minor Canons of St. Pauls of a pipe from the conduit in Paternoster Row', C.T.G., 3, 1836, p.80-81.

BROCKETT, W. H. 'Early records of Sherburn Hospital, Co. Durham, with a catalogue of its estates in Gateshead', T.G., 3, 1858, p.563-8.

F., T. 'Documents relating to the school and guild at Stratford-upon-Avon', C.T.G., 3, 1836, p.81-4. [15th c.]

T., B. C. 'Catalogue of the high stewards of the Borough of Malmesbury, Wilts', C.T.G., 6, 1840, p.297-8. [17-18th c.]

'Petition to Parliament from the borough of Wotton Basset, in the reign of Charles I, relative to the right of the burgesses to free common of pasture in Fasterne Great Park', T.G., 3, 1858, p.22-5. [Wiltshire]

9. ECCLESIASTICAL ESTATES

G., G. C. 'Charters in the muniment room of the Prefecture of St. Lo, Department of La Manche, Normandy, relating to English churches', T.G., 1, 1846, p.194-6. [Southampton, Exeter and Bath; 12-13th c]

M. 'Valuation of the estates of the bishopricks of England and Wales in 1647', C.T.G., 3, 1836, p.19-48.

M., F. 'Account of the sale of bishops' lands between the years 1647 and 1651', C.T.G., 1, 1834, p.1-8, 122-7, & 284-92. [Gives lands, purchasers, and prices]

P., & M. 'List of monastic cartularies at present existing, or which are known to have existed since the dissolution of religious houses', C.T.G., 1, 1834, p.73-9, 197-208, & 399-410; 2, 1835, p.102-14. See also 'Additions and corrections to the list of cartularies', C.T.G., 2, 1835, p.400; 4, 1837, p.403.

BRISTOL

See Glastonbury

BULLINGTON

G., ed. 'Covenant between the Convent of Bullington, Co. Lincoln, and William Burgh, esq., for the reception of his daughter as a nun in 1479', C.T.G., 4, 1837, p.90.

BURNHAM

N., J. G. 'Charters relating to the Abbey of Burnham, Co. Buckingham', C.T.G., 8, 1843, p.120-31.

CHERTSEY

OLIVER, Geo. 'Register of Chertsey Abbey', C.T.G., 4, 1837, p.164-8. [Surrey; 14th c.]

CROKESDEN

M., F. 'Extracts from the annals of Crokesden Abbey, Co. Stafford', C.T.G., 2, 1835, p.297-310.

DURHAM

HODGSON, John. 'Abstracts of original charters in the treasury of the Dean and Chapter of Durham, respecting religious institutions and private property in Newcastle-upon-Tyne', C.T.G., 4, 1837, p.81-90. [13-14th. c.]

EXETER

P. 'List of charters in the cartulary of St. Nicholas at Exeter', C.T.G., 1, 1834, p.60-65, 184-9, 250-4, & 374-88.

GLASTONBURY

N., J. G. 'Release of the Prior and Fraternity of Kalendaries in Bristol, of property in Bristol, to the Abbey of Glastonbury, 1466', C.T.G., 4, 1837, p.244-6.

GOKEWELL

L., L. B. ' Charters relating to the family of De Alta Ripa, and nunnery of Gokewell, Co. Lincoln', C.T.G., 4, 1837, p.241-2. [12th c.]

GRANDMONT

E., H. 'Survey of Grandmont Priory, in Yorkshire', C.T.G., 2, 1835, p.365-7. [16th c.]

HASTINGS

N., J. G. 'Charters relating to the Priory of Hastings, Sussex', C.T.G., 6, 1840, p.101-8.

HAUGHMOND

M., G. 'Abbats of Haghmon, Co. Salop, and extracts from the cartulary of that abbey', C.T.G., 1, 1874, p.362-74.

HEREFORD

S., G. S. 'Charter of William de Ebroicis, or Devereaux, granting to the Priory of Hereford, his land in Balingham, Co. Hereford', C.T.G., 4, 1837, p.246-7. [13th c.]

HEXHAM

M., & N. 'Abstract of a cartulary of Hexham Abbey', C.T.G., 6, 1840, p.38-46.

IPSWICH

L., L. B. 'Grant of Sprouton, Co. Suffolk, by Rodbert de Blanchville to the Canons of Ipswich', C.T.G., 4, 1837, p.242-3. [c. 12th c.]

JARROW

HODGSON, John. 'Collections respecting the monastery of Jarrow', C.T.G., 1, 1834, p.66-73.

HODGSON, John. 'Collections respecting the monastery and parish of Jarrow, in the county of Durham; the chapelry of Heworth, and the chapelry of South Shields', C.T.G., 2, 1835, p.40-48.

JERUSALEM

C., G. T. 'Charter by John Earl of Moreton, afterwards King John, to the Master and Brethren of the Temple of Salom, in Jerusalem', T.G., 1, 1846, p.321-3.

LEAMINGTON HASTINGS

N., J. G. 'Particulars of the advowson of Leamington Hastings, in Warwickshire, written temp. James I', C.T.G., 1, 1874, p.293-4.

LITTLE MALVERN

S., G. S. 'Charters relating to the gift of a virgate of land in Knightwick, Co. Worcester, to the Priory of Little Malvern, by Simon de Mans temp Hen. I', C.T.G., 4, 1837, p.238-40. [12th c.]

LONDON

L., L. B. 'Lease from Peter, Prior of Christ Church, London, of land in the parish of St. Michael Bassishaw, temp Richard I', C.T.G., 4, 1837, p.310-11. [12th c.]

MARGAM

T., I. M. 'The abbots of Margam Abbey, Glamorganshire', C.T.G., 6, 1840, p.188-9.

T., J. M. 'Documents relating to Lanveithin and Resolven, estates of the Abbey of Margam', C.T.G., 5, 1838, p.18-20.

MORFIELD

E., H. 'Particular of the cell of Morfield in Shropshire, in 1545', C.T.G., 2, 1835, p.289-91.

NEATH

'Charter of John Lord Mowbray, Lord of Gower, dated in 1334, confirming two charters of Henry Earl of Warwick, and other rights and privileges to the abbey of Neath, Glamorgan', C.T.G., 4, 1837, p.29-32.

NEWSTEAD

L., B. L. 'Charters relating to the lands of the Priory of Newstead in Cadney, at Hibaldstow in Lincolnshire', C.T.G., 5, 1838, p.157-60.

SAINT ALBANS

H., W. H. 'On the Archdeaconry of St. Albans, with a list of archdeacons from 1415 to 1539, being antecedent to the list given by Newcourt', C.T.G., 7, 1841, p.302-3.

SAINT ANDREW'S

S., T. 'Ground plan and charters of St. Andrew's Priory in the parish of Marrigg, North Riding, Co. Ebor', C.T.G., 5, 1838, p.157-60. [Includes pedigree of Powlett of Marrick, 17-18th c., and Uvedale of Marrick, 16th c.]

SAINT ASAPH

W. 'Index registri et rentalis ecclesiae cathedralis Sancti Asaph, in Wallia', C.T.G., 2, 1835, p.253-4. [Medieval]

W. 'Summa libri rubei Asaphensis communiterdicti, "Llyfr coch Asaph", exscript. ex originale 26 Octobris 1602', C.T.G., 2, 1835, p.255-79. [The red book of St. Asaph: an index to a lost medieval act book]

SCARBOROUGH

L., L. B. 'Grant of Matilda, widow of Adam Brus of Pickering, of land in Scarborough to the Friars Minor of that town, 1323', C.T.G., 4, 1837, p.312.

SHREWSBURY

P. 'Extracts from the cartulary of St. Peter's Abbey at Shrewsbury, comprising an index of the charters', C.T.G., 1, 1834, p.23-8 & 190-6.

TALLINGTON

'Grant of the church of Tallington, Co. Linc., to the Priory of Belvoir, by William de Albineio Brito', C.T.G., 1, 1834, p.32-3. [12th c.]

THORNEY

M., ed. 'Saxon charters to Thorney Abbey, in Cambridgeshire', C.T.G., 4, 1837, p.54-9.

TICHFIELD

M., F. 'Abbats of Tichfield Abbey, in Hampshire', C.T.G., 1, 1834, p.14-16.

TYWARDREATH

O., G. 'List of priors, and extracts from the calendar, of Tywardreath Priory, Cornwall', C.T.G., 3, 1836, p.106-11.

WALTHAM

N., J. G. ed. 'Charters relating to the estates of the Abbey of Waltham at Alrichesey, now Arlesey, Co. Bedford', C.T.G., 6, 1840, p.196-236.

WINCHCOMBE

P. 'List of charters in the Winchcombe cartularies, in the possession of Lord Sherborne', C.T.G., 2, 1835, p.16-39. [Gloucestershire]

WINCHESTER

N., J. G. 'Indenture of the transfer of the patronage of the Hospital of St. Cross by Winchester, from the Prior of St. John of Jerusalem to Richard Bishop of Winchester in 1185', C.T.G., 3, 1836, p.174-7.

YEOVIL

N., J. G. 'Account of the proctors of the church of Yeovil, Co. Somerset, 36 Hen. VI, 1457-8', C.T.G., 3, 1836, p.134-41.

10. GENERAL HISTORY AND TOPOGRAPHY

B., W. D. Addenda and corrigenda, T.G., 2, 1853, p.539-50. [Letter to the editor correcting the author's own contributions]

BURN, John Southerden. 'Sponsalia', C.T.G., 3, 1836, p.320-6. [Obsolete marriage law and custom]

F., J. F. 'Exactions incident to tenures in Ireland', T.G., 3, 1858, p.123-46.

N., J. G. 'Pensions of the Court of Wards, 1623', C.T.G., 8, 1843, p. 38-9.

S., C., 'Letter from Cardinal Wolsey to Count Beaumont, respecting stone for building his colleges at Ipswich and Oxford', C.T.G., 1, 1874, p.241-2.

Y., C. G. 'A roll of the band of gentlemen pensioners in 1608', C.T.G., 6, 1840, p.192-3.

Addenda', C.T.G., 3, 1836, p.401-4.

'Additions and corrections', C.T.G., 2, 1835, p.398-9; 4, 1837, p.396-402; 5, 1838, p.400-2; 6, 1840, p.400; 7, 1841, p.400-3; 8, 1843, p.408-13.

'The ancient Earldoms of England', T.G., 1, 1846, p.1-28. [Primarily concerned with the Earldom of Lincoln, 11-12th c.]

'The bibliography of genealogy and topography', T.G., 1, 1846, p.83-112. [Publications of 1842]

BERKSHIRE

B., W. H. 'Descent of the estate of Clifton-Ferry in the parish of Long-Wittenham, Berks.', C.T.G., 1, 1874, p.239-41. [Medieval]

G., C. C. 'An account of the foundation of the chapel, chauntry and guild of Maidenhead, in the county of Berks., with a few particulars relating to the parishes of Cookham and Bray, in which that town is situated', C.T.G., 5, 1838, p.47-67 & 158-88. [Includes list of Cookham vicars, some Cookham monumental inscriptions, and a list of Bray vicars]

BUCKINGHAMSHIRE

B., W. H. 'The customs of the manor of Crendon, in Buckinghamshire, 1558', C.T.G., 5, 1838, p.200-1.

CAMBRIDGESHIRE

G., G. C. 'An account of the appropriation of the rectory of Eltisley, Cambridgeshire, to Denney Abbey, together with a list of the incumbents, notices of monumental inscriptions, and of the descent of the manors in that parish', C.T.G., 6, 1840, p.362-9.

CHESHIRE

N., J. 'Chronicles of Thelwall, Co. Chester, with notices of the successive lords of that manor, their family descent, etc', T.G., 1, 1846, p.379-94 & 431-68.

CO. CORK

C., R. 'Testimony to the exemption of Skiddy's Lands, near Cork, from the impositions of coyne and livery, &c., given in the 37 Hen. VIII', T.G., 3, 1858, p.371-4.

HINGSTON, James. 'Statistical account of the Diocese of Cloyne, compiled in the year 1774', T.G., 3, 1858, p.303-25.

T., S. 'Case of the Rev. Paul Limerick, rector of Kilmore, Co. Cork, as to the glebe of Crookhaven', T.G., 2, 1853, p.344-56.

DERBYSHIRE

C., G. T. 'Notices of Dethick and Ashover, Co. Derby, and the families of Dethick and Babington', C.T.G., 2, 1835, p.94-101. [Includes monumental inscriptions]

'Catalogue of the collections for a history of the county of Derby formed by Samuel Pegge, Ll. D., rector of Whittington', C.T.G., 3, 1836, p.240-9.

DEVON

STEINMAN, G. Steinman. 'Some account of the Isle of Lundy', C.T.G., 4, 1837, p.313-30.

ESSEX

N., J. G. 'Particulars of the manor of Gaines in Upminster, Essex, in 1722', C.T.G., 1, 1874, p.331-2.

P., A. 'Notices of Stanway, in the Hundred of Lexden, Essex', C.T.G., 7, 1841, p.273-8.

GLAMORGANSHIRE

'Decree of John, Bishop of Llandaff, regarding the tithes of the parish of Llangeinwr, Co. Glamorgan, 1466', T.G., 2, 1853, p.253-6.

GLOUCESTERSHIRE

G., S. 'Account of Lechlade Bridge, Gloucestershire', C.T.G., 1, 1874, p.320-4.

'Indenture enumerating various lands in Cirencester, 4 Hen VIII 1489', T.G., 3, 1858, p.95-6. [Actually 4 Henry VII]

HAMPSHIRE

M. 'Burning of the Queen's store-houses at Portsmouth in 1557', C.T.G., 2, 1835, p.251-2. [Certificate by the mayor and burgesses]

HEREFORDSHIRE

P., R. B. 'Grant to the almshouse of St. Ethelbert in Hereford, by Isabel Cantilupe, wife of Stephen de Ebroicis and of Ralph Penebruge', C.T.G., 2, 1835, p.250. [12-13th c.]

KENT

STEINMAN, G. Steinman. 'Some account of the manor of Apuldrefield in the parish of Cudham, Kent', T.G., 3, 1858, p.1-21 & 178-222. [Includes medieval pedigree of Apuldrefield, and 16-17th c. pedigree of Lennard]

'Survey of the marshes on the River Medway, temp. Hen. VIII or Edw. VI', T.G., 2, 1853, p.447-9.

LANCASHIRE

P. 'Boundaries of Pendleton, Co. Lancaster', C.T.G., 1, 1874, p.248.

LEICESTERSHIRE

N., J. G. 'Abstract of documents relative to the manor of Gumley, Co Leicester, and to freeschools at Little Harrowden, Pitchley and Irtlingborough, Co. Northampton, and Hallaton Co. Leicester', C.T.G., 3, 1836, p.330-2.

LONDON AND MIDDLESEX

M. 'Syon monastery, Middlesex', C.T.G., 1, 1834, p.29-32. [Notes on its rule]

Y., C. G. 'Strangers resident in London in 1595', C.T.G., 8, 1843, p.205-9.

'Charter relative to a garden near the gaol of London, and seven acres at Edmonton, circa 1180', C.T.G., 3, 1836, p.285.

NORFOLK

N., J. G. 'Views in Norfolk', C.T.G., 8, 1843, p.117-9. [Contents of a volume of drawings]

P., A. 'Extracts from the topographical collections of Sir Henry Calthorpe, Knt., temp Charles I, relating to several parishes in the county of Norfolk', C.T.G., 7, 1841, p.197-210. See also correspondence concerning Ufford in T.G., 1, 1846, p.299-300. [Burgh St. Margarets; Stiffkey; Acle; Aldeby; Hadiscoe Thorpe; Wiveton]

NORTHAMPTONSHIRE

See under Leicestershire

SHROPSHIRE

DUKES, Thomas Farmer. 'Collections for the history of Shropshire', C.T.G., 1, 1874, p.227-38. [From the collections of Edward Lloyd; concerns Adderley, Caux Castle, Ellesmere and Pontesbury; medieval]

M., G. 'Early deeds relating to Shropshire', C.T.G., 5, 1838, p.175-81.

STAFFORDSHIRE

M., ed. 'Leland's unpublished notes of Staffordshire families, and an unpublished fragment of his itinerary', C.T.G., 3, 1836, p.338-44.

SUFFOLK

G. 'Grant of lands at Pridinton, in Hawkedon, Suffolk, from Richard Fitz Gilbert, Earl of Clare, to the Abbey of St. Edmund', C.T.G., 1, 1874, p.388-9.

P., A. 'Topographical notices of the parishes of Ampton, Harkstead, and Livermere Parva, Suffolk', C.T.G., 7, 1841, p.292-301.

SURREY

B., J. 'Abstract of a deed of feoffment relating to "The Garrett", near Wandsworth, in the county of Surrey, the scene of the celebrated mock election', C.T.G., 5, 1838, p.91-3. [1564]

C., G. R. 'Abstract of sundry deeds relating to houses in the parishes of St. Saviour and St. Olave, Southwark, in Com. Surrey, formerly called the Dolphin and the Bear Taverns, at the foot of London Bridge, with notices of the families of Leke and Middleton of Southwark', C.T.G., 5, 1838, p.45-61. [Includes pedigree of Leake, 16-17th c.; will of John Midleton, 1582, and 15 deeds]

C., G. R. 'Some particulars of the Abbot of Battle's Inn, in the parish of Saint Olave, Southwark, and of the manor of the Maze in the same parish, and of some of the owners of that manor', C.T.G., 8, 1843, p.247-62.

L., C. E. ed. 'Church goods of the county of Surrey, 7 Edw. VI (from the Loseley Mss)', C.T.G., 8, 1843, p.262-3.

STEINMAN, G. Steinman. 'An account of the manor of Haling, in the parish of Croydon, Surrey, and of some of its possessors', C.T.G., 3, 1836, p.1-18. [Includes pedigrees of Warham, 15-16th c., Gardiner, 16-17th c., and Parker and Hamond, 17-18th c., also a survey of the manor, 1531, and an extent, 1592]

STEINMAN, G. Steinman. 'Some account of the manors of Whitehorse, Croham and Norbury, in the parish of Croydon, Surrey, and a pedigree of Elmerugge', C.T.G., 5, 1838, p.161-74. [Pedigree of Elmerugge of Worcester and Croham, 13-16th c.]

WARWICKSHIRE

READER, W. 'Deeds relating to St. John's Hospital, Coventry', C.T.G., 2, 1835, p.152-9.

R., W. ed. 'Warwickshire noblemen and gentlemen in 1733 and 1742', C.T.G., 8, 1843, p.361-3.

S., W. 'Catalogue of residents in the county of Warwick, in the reign of Elizabeth, by Henry Ferrers of Baddesley, esq', C.T.G., 8, 1843, p.298-308.

W., R. B. 'Ordination of the chapel of Bishopton in the parish of Stratford upon Avon, made by Sir William de Bishopton, Knt., in the presence of Maugerius, Bishop of Worcester, in the reign of King John, about the year 1200', C.T.G., 5, 1838, p.399-400.

YORKSHIRE

A., G. J. 'Descent of some of the principal property in Romanby township, in the parish of North Allerton, North Riding of Yorkshire', T.G., 1, 1846, p.323-9. See also p.496.

BRUCE, William D. 'An account of the parish of Newton Kyme, in the county of York', T.G., 1, 1846, p.500-5.

B., W. D. 'Some notice of the descent of the principal estates in the parish of Kirby-Wiske, in the North Riding of Yorkshire', T.G., 1, 1846, p.294-9.

HUNTER, Joseph. 'Dewsbury, in the Archbishopric of York: its ecclesiastical history', C.T.G., 1, 1834, p.149-68.

T., J. F. 'Charters relating to Elslack and Glusburne, in Craven, Co. York, with a pedigree of their descent in the families of Darell, Marton, De Alta Ripa (or Dautrey), Radcliffe, and Malhome; and pedigrees of Vavasur, Reuell, Sutton, Wratham, Clusburne, etc', C.T.G., 6, 1840, p.123-47 & 301-33. [13-17th c; 196 deeds]

'A description of Cleveland, in a letter addressed by H. Tr. to Sir Thomas Chaloner', T.G., 2, 1853, p.403-32.

'Manor of Hutton Bonville in Birkby parish, Allertonshire, North Riding of Yorkshire', T.G., 1, 1846, 509-12.

AUTHOR INDEX

INDEX OF FAMILY NAMES

INDEX OF PLACES

ENGLAND

UNLOCATED

WALES

IRELAND

OVERSEAS

THE ANCESTOR

a quarterly review of county and
family history, heraldry and
antiquities.

12 vols.

Westminster: Archibold Constable & Co.,
1902-5.

THE ANCESTOR

INTRODUCTION

The Ancestor ran for 4 years under the editorship of Oswald Barron. The aim of the journal was to present scholarly articles on genealogy and allied subjects, and well over fifty per cent of its columns are occupied by accounts of particular families with a bias towards the medieval period. J. H. Round, and other contributors of similar bent, paid particular attention to the debunking of genealogical myths - especially those concerned with claims to have 'come over with the Conqueror'.

In addition to family histories, the Ancestor included articles on heraldry, art and general history, together with reviews, letters to the editor, and a few extracts from historical records - especially wills. The aim of this bibliography is to assist the genealogist or local historian in identifying material relevant to his research. Names of authors and the titles of their works, are given exactly as they occur in the journal. An attempt has been made to indicate the county and the period to which an article pertains, if the information is not obvious from the title. Letters to the editor are cited seperately only if they provide substantive information. Where they refer to other articles in the Ancestor they are cited with the relevant article. Reviews are listed alphabetically by author; reviewers names, where given, are noted in brackets. In general, I have not checked citations to books reviewed or given in the Ancestor against the actual book, although this was necessary in a few instances.

Detailed indexes of names were published by the Ancestor for vols. 1-4, 5-8, and 9-12, and provide a useful suupplement to the present work. They will usually be found with the journal.

Stuart A. Raymond

1. FAMILY HISTORY

B., G. 'Notes on some Durham families', Anc., 5, Apr. 1903, p.92-8. [Includes pedigrees of Dale of Dalton & Tunstall, Goodchild of Pallion, Holme of Wearmouth, Laurence of Bishops Wearmouth, Twentyman of Middle Herrington, & Jackson of West Rainton]

OBREEN, H. G. A. 'Notes from the Netherlands, 1: the nobility of the Netherlands', Anc., 9, April 1904, p.210-13. [Notes on families of English and Scottish origin in 1903]

'A royal pedigree and a picture of the Black Prince', Anc., 11, Oct., 1904, p.158-60.

ANGELO

SWYNNERTON, Charles. 'The Angelo family,' Anc., 8, Jan., 1904, p.1-72. See also letter from John P. Steel, Anc. 10, July 1904, p.223. [Italian; Includes pedigrees, 18-19th c.]

BACHEPUZ

ROUND, J. Horace. 'A Bachepuz charter', Anc., 12, Dec., 1904, p.152-5. [Derbyshire & Berkshire]

BAILDON

BAILDON, W. Paley. 'Ancestors' letters, 1', Anc., 1, April 1902, p.160-5. [Baildon family, Yorkshire, 16-17th c.]

BARKER

BARRON, Oswald. 'The gentility of Richard Barker', Anc., 2, July 1902, p.48-53. [Norfolk., 16th c.]

BARNHAM

LENNARD, T. Barrett.'A copy of an original manuscript of Sir Francis Barnham, formerly of Boughton Monchelsea, knight, now in the possession of his descendant Sir Thomas Rider, knight', Anc., 9, April 1904, p.191-209. [Boughton Monchelsea, Kent; Barnham family history, 16-17th c.]

BARON

'The Huguenot families in England, II: the Barons', Anc., 3, Oct., 1902, p.105-17.[of Boston, Lincolnshire; pedigree, 16-17th c.]

BARROW

ROUND, J. Horace. 'An early citizen squire', Anc., 2, July, 1902, p.58-62. [Barrow family of London; includes pedigree, 11-13th c.]

BASSET

BARRON, Oswald. 'Our oldest families, XII: the Bassets', Anc., 11, Oct., 1904, p.55-60. [Cornwall; 12-19th c.]

BATTYE

'A family of soldiers', Anc., 1, April 1902, p.264(f). [Pedigree of Battye, various counties, 18-19th c.]

BEKYNGHAM

See Hawtrey

BERESFORD

ROUND, J. Horace. 'The Beresfords' origin and arms', Anc., 12, Dec., 1904, p.169-77. [Staffordshire; medieval]

BERKELEY

BARRON, Oswald. 'Our oldest families, X: the Berkeleys', Anc., 8, Jan., 1904, p.73-81. [Gloucestershire; 11-19th c.]

BLOYOU

TAYLOR, Thomas. 'Blohin: his descendants and lands', Anc., 9, April 1904, p.20-27. See also letter from Extraneous, Anc. 10, July 1904, p.226. [Cornwall; Descent through Bloyou and Carminow; medieval]

BRAY

'The Brays of Shere', Anc., 6, July 1903, p.1-10. [Surrey, 15-19th c.]

BUXTON

RYE, Walter. 'Buxton of Shadwell Court', Anc., 6, July 1903, p.11-18. [Norfolk; medieval]

CAREW

ROUND, J. Horace. 'The origin of the Carews', Anc., 5, Apr. 1903, p.19-53. [Medieval; includes pedigrees.]

CARMINOW

See Bloyou

CARTERET

'Our oldest families, IV: Carteret', Anc., 3, Oct., 1902, p.218-22. [Jersey; 12-18th c.]

CARTWRIGHT

BARRON, Oswald. 'The Cartwrights', Anc., 10, July 1904, p.1-12. [Various counties; 16-19th c.]

CLINTON

EXUL. 'Cases from the early Chancery proceedings, 1: the Lady Clinton', Anc., 8, Jan., 1904, p.167-201. [Medieval]

EXUL. 'The Clinton family, II', Anc., 10, July 1904, p.32-51. [Warwickshire; Medieval]

ROUND, J. Horace. 'A great marriage settlement', Anc., 11, Oct., 1904, p.1543-7. [Agnes, daughter of Roger, Earl of Warwick=Geoffrey de Clinton; 12th c.]

COMYN

ROUND, J. Horace. 'Comyn and Valoignes', Anc., 11, Oct., 1904, p.129-35.

COSTEBADIES

LART, Chas. E. 'The families of the strangers: the Costebadies', Anc., 7, Oct., 1903, p.45-52. [Huguenot family]

COULTHART

BARRON, Oswald. 'The bonny house of Coulthart: an old story retold', Anc., 4, Jan., 1903, p.61-80. [Wigtownshire; 'exposure' of a false pedigree]

CRESSY

MADDISON, A. K. 'The Cressy family', Anc. 9, April 1904, p.235. [Lincolnshire, 17th c.; letter to the editor]

CUMINS

ROUND, J. Horace. 'The Cumins of Snitterfield', Anc., 9, April 1904, p.146-9. [Warwickshire & Scotland; medieval]

D'AUBENEY

ROUND, J. Horace. 'A D'Aubeney cadet', Anc., 12, Dec., 1904, p.149-51. [Wiltshire; 12-13th c.]

DELAFIELD

BARRON, Oswald. 'The Delafields and the Empire', Anc., 11, Oct., 1904, p.97-128. [13-19th c.]

DENSILL

HUGHES, Michael W. 'Corrections and additions to the pedigree of Densill', Anc., 12, Dec., 1904, p.118-24. [Cornwall; medieval]

DIGBY

DIGBY, H. M. 'George Digby, Earl of Bristol', Anc., 11, Oct., 1904, p.71-88. [Leicestershire; 17th c.]

ESMONT

ROUND, J. Horace. 'An 'authoritative' ancestor', Anc., 1, April 1902, p.189-94. [Lincolnshire; 12th c.]

EXELBY

BARRON, Oswald. 'The gentility of William Exelby', Anc., 3, Oct., 1902, p.127-31. [Middlesex; 16-17th c.]

FANE

WEBBER-INCLEDON, L. C. 'Letters of the Fanes and Incledons', Anc., 11, Oct., 1904, p.136-9. [Devon; 17th c.]

BARRON, Oswald. 'The Fanes', Anc., 12, Dec., 1904, p.4-17. [15-19th c; various counties]

FERRERS

FERRERS, Cecil S. F. 'William Ferrers of Taplow, Bucks.' Anc., 8, Jan. 1904, p.226-7. [15th c., Letter to the editor]

FISHER

FYSHER, Jhon. '[Letter to the editor concerning errors of the Heralds]' Anc., 7, Oct. 1903, p.263-5.

FITZGERALD

ROUND, J. Horace. 'The origin of the Fitzgeralds', Anc., 1, April 1902, p.119-26, & 2, July 1902, p.91-98. [Ireland; includes 12th c. pedigree]

FITZWILLIAM

BARRON, Oswald. 'Our oldest families, XIV: the Fitzwilliams', Anc., 12, Dec., 1904, p.111-7. [11-18th c.]

FREKE

FREKE, Ralph, & FREKE, John. 'A pedigree or genealogy of the family of ye Frekes for nearly 200 years ...'. Anc., 10, July 1904, p.179-212, & 11, Oct., 1904, p.33-54. [Dorset and Somerset; pedigrees, 16-18th c.]

FRY

FRY, E. A. 'A Kentish Chancery suit', Anc., 2, July 1902, p.204(f). [Fry pedigree, 17th c.]

GIFFARD

ROUND, J. Horace. 'Giffard of Fonthill Giffard', Anc., 6, July 1903, p.137-47. [Wiltshire; medieval]

G., H. F. 'Earldom of Buckingham', Anc., 12, Jan. 1905, p.192-4. [Giffard family; medieval; letter to the editor]

GOWRIE

LANG, Andrew. 'The Gowrie conspiracy and the Gowrie arms', Anc., 2, July 1902, p.54-7. See also author's letter, Anc. 4, Jan.1903, p.254-5. [Scotland, 16th c.]

GRENVILLE

TAYLOR, Thomas. 'The genesis of a myth', Anc., 3, Oct., 1902, p.98-104. [Grenfell or Grenville, Cornwall, 18-19th c.]

GREYSTOKE

WILSON, James. 'Some extinct Cumberland families, IV: the Greystokes', Anc., 6, July 1903, p.121-34. [Includes pedigree, 12-16th c.]

GROSVENOR

BIRD, W. H. B. 'The Grosvenor myth', Anc., 1, April 1902, p.166-88. [Cheshire; medieval]

See also Lostock

HARRIS

MALMESBURY, Earl of. 'Some anecdotes of the Harris family', Anc., 1, April 1902, p.1-27. [Wiltshire; 17-18th c.]

HAWTREY

EXUL. 'Cases from the early Chancery proceedings, II: Hawtrey v. Bekyngham', Anc., 11, Oct., 1904, p.191-6. [Oxfordshire; 15th c.]

HEREFORD

HERFORD, A. F. 'The Hereford family of Plymouth', Anc., 7, Oct., 1903, p.71-4. [16th c.]

HERVEY

WORTHAM, R. Hale. 'An ancestral scandal', Anc., 5, Apr. 1903, p.73-80. [Hervey of Thurleigh, Bedfordshire; includes pedigree, 15-17th c.]

HOLMES

'TEMPLAR'. 'The Holmes of Wearmouth', Anc., 2, July 1902, p.234-5. [Co. Durham; letter to the editor]

INCLEDON

See Fane

JACKSON

BEWLEY, Sir Edmund T. 'The Jacksons in Ireland', Anc., 7, Oct., 1903, p.67-70. [17th c.]

PIGOTT, William Jackson. 'Sir Anthony Jackson, knight: a herald of the Civil War', Anc., 6, July 1903, p.89-91. [Yorkshire]

JERNINGHAM

ROUND, J. Horace. 'The Jerninghams', Anc., 12, Dec., 1904, p.186-7. [Medieval]

JERVOISE

JERVOISE, F. H. T. 'The Jervoises of Herriard and Britford', Anc., 3, Oct. 1902, p.1-13 [Hampshire & Wiltshire; 16-17th c; includes an undated inventory of Sir Richard Poulett of Herryott, Hants.]

JOHNSTON

JOHNSTON, Geo. Harvey. 'John Johnston', Anc., 7, Jan. 1904, p.223-4. See also 10, July 1904, p.224-6; 11, Oct. 1904, p.199-200. [Letters to the editor re Annandale peerage case]

KNIGHT

'The Knights of Chawton', Anc., 4, Jan., 1903, p.1-6. [Hampshire; 16-19th c.]

KNIGHTLEY

KNIGHTLEY, Lady, & BARRON, Oswald. 'The Knightleys of Fawsley', Anc., 2, July 1902, p.1-13. [Northamptonshire; medieval-19th c.]

'Ancestors' letters, no.2: Edmund Knightley and Dame Jane Knightley', Anc., 2, July 1902, p.121-2. [16th c.]

LANGTON

BARRON, Oswald. 'Our oldest families, VIII: the Langtons', Anc., 7, Oct., 1903, p.166-9. [Lincolnshire]

LAMBERT

ROUND, J. Horace. 'The tale of a great forgery', Anc., 3, Oct., 1902, p.14-35. [Lambert of Surrey and Yorkshire; medieval]

LEIGHTON

'Our oldest families, V: the Leightons', Anc., 4, Jan., 1903, p.115-8. See also letter from J. Horace Round, 5, April 1903, p.221-2. [Shropshire; pedigree, 12-15th c.]

LEVINGTON

WILSON, James. 'Some extinct Cumberland families, II: the Levingtons', Anc., 3, Oct., 1902, p.80-84. [13th c. pedigree]

LOSTOCK

BIRD, W. H. B. 'Lostock and the Grosvenors', Anc., 2, July 1902, p.148-55. [Cheshire; 13-14th c.]

LUPUS

TAYLOR, Tho. 'Lupus', Anc. 5, April 1903, p.224-5. [Cornwall; medieval; letter to the editor]

LYTE

MAXWELL-LYTE, Sir H. 'Heraldic glass from Lytes Cary, Co. Somerset', Anc., 1, April 1902, p.104-11. [Lyte family; 16th c]

MALET

'The representation of the Malets', Anc., 11, Oct. 1904, p.197-9. [Malet of Iddesleigh, Devon, 16th c.; letter to the editor]

MASSINGBERD

MASSINGBERD, W. O. 'The Massingberds of Sutterton, Gunby, and Ormsby', Anc., 7, Oct., 1903, p.1-14. See also letter from Geo. J. Armytage, Anc., 8, Jan. 1904, p.225. [Lincolnshire; 12-19th c.]

MAUDIT

ROUND, J. Horace. 'Maudit of Hartley Maudit', Anc., 5, Apr. 1903, p.207-10. [Hampshire; 12th c.]

MENTEITH

BLAYDES, F. A. 'The Earls of Menteith', Anc., 4, Jan., 1903, p.81-7. [Scotland]

MONSON-WATSON

WISE, Chas. 'The death of Thomas, third Earl of Rockingham, and the Monson-Watson succession to his estates', Anc., 7, Oct., 1903, p.54-8. [Kent; 18th c.]

MONTAGU

DORLING, E. E. 'Notes on the Montagu monument in Salisbury Cathedral', Anc., 6, July 1903, p.46-8. [Sir John Montagu, 1396.]

MULTON

MASSINGBERD, W. O. 'Notes on the pedigree of Multon of Frampton, Co. Lincoln', Anc., 2, July 1902, p.205-7. [14th c. pedigree]

NEVILL

BARRON, Oswald. 'Our oldest families, no. VII: the Nevills', Anc., 6, July 1903, p.197-202.

NICOLLS

BIRD, W. H. B. 'Doctor and patient in 1621', Anc., 3, Oct., 1902, p.36-40. [Nicolls of Northamptonshire and Leicestershire; 16th c.]

OGLE

BARRON, Oswald. 'Our oldest families, XI: the Ogles', Anc., 9, April 1904, p.181-6. [Northumberland; 12-19th c.]

OKEOVER

B[ARRON], O[swald]. 'Our oldest families, VI: the Okeovers', p.191-4. [Staffordshire, 12-14th c.]

PEMBERTON

SIMPSON, C. E. Pinckney. 'Durham families', Anc., 6, July 1903, p.206-7. [Pemberton family of Aislabie, Co. Durham; letter to the editor]

PENTHENY

See Repenteneye

PETT

BURKE, H. Farnham, & BARRON, Oswald. 'The builders of the navy: a genealogy of the family of Pett', Anc., 10, July 1904, p.147-77. See also letter to ed. Anc. 12, Jan. 1905, p.194-5. [London, Kent & Essex; 16-17th c]

POLLOCK

'A family of lawyers', Anc., 4, Jan., 1903, p.142f. [Pollock pedigree; various counties]

POPHAM

ROUND, J. Horace. 'The rise of the Pophams', Anc., 7, Oct., 1903, p.59-66. [Hampshire; medieval]

POULETT

See Jervoise

PRESTON

RYE, Walter. 'A family legend: the emerald ring of the Preston family', Anc., 2, July 1902, p.82-90. [Suffolk; 16-17th c. pedigree]

REPENTENEYE

RYE, Walter. 'De Pentheny-O'Kelly of Tara', Anc., 5, April, 1903, p.220-1. [Letter to the editor]

RUSSELL

READE, Aleyn Lyell. 'Russell family of New Bond Street', Anc., 5, Apr. 1903, p.203-6.

SAMBORNE

SAMBORN, V. S. 'A possible Samborne ancestry', Anc., 11, Oct., 1904, p.61-70. [Wiltshire, Somerset, & Berkshire; 12-15th c.]

SANDYS

WILSON, James. 'The arms of the Sandys of Cumberland', Anc., 3, Oct., 1902, p.85. [16th c.]

SCHOTT

SCOTT, S. H. 'An old German family history', Anc., 5, Apr. 1903, p.169-74. [Schott family, 15-19th c.]

SHERIDAN

SHERIDAN, Wilfred. 'Some account of the Sheridan family', Anc., 9, April 1904, p.1-5. See also letter by W. Le Fanu, Anc., 10 July 1904, p.227. [17-19th c.]

SHIRLEY

'Our oldest families, III: Shirley', Anc., 3, Oct., 1902, p.214-8. [12-18th c.]

SWYNNERTON

SWYNNERTON, Chas. 'On some forgotten Swynnertons of the fourteenth century', Anc., 7, Oct., 1903, p.216-43. See also letter from G. Cavenagh-Mainwaring, with reply, Anc., 8, Jan. 1904, p.228-32. [Staffordshire; includes pedigree, 13-17th c.]

SWYNNERTON, Charles. 'Two ancient petitions from the Public Record Office', Anc., 6, July 1903, p.66-71. [Concerning Roger de Swynnerton, 1320, Staffordshire]

TICHBORNE

B[ARRON], O[swald]. 'Our oldest families, II: Tichborne', Anc., 2, July 1902, p.114-9. [Hampshire; 12th c.]

TILLIOL

WILSON, James. 'Some extinct Cumberland families, III: the Tilliols', Anc., 4, Jan., 1903, p.88-100. See also letter from J. Horace Round, Anc., 6, July 1903, p.206. [Pedigree, 12-15th c.]

TRAFFORD

BIRD, W. H. B. 'The Trafford legend', Anc., 9, April 1904, p.65-82, & 10, July 1904, p.73-82. [Lancashire; medieval]

BIRD, W. H. B. 'Mr. Round and the Trafford legend', Anc., 12, Dec., 1904, p.42-51.

ROUND, J. Horace. 'Mr. Bird and the Trafford legend', Anc., 12, Dec., 1904, p.52-5.

TRYON

'The Huguenot families in England, 1: the Tryons', Anc., 2, July 1902, p.175-86. See also letter by C. F. D. Sperling, Anc., 4, Jan. 1903, p.256-7. [London, Essex and Northamptonshire]

VALOIGNES

See Comyn

VANDEPUT

B., O. 'The Huguenot families in England, III: the Vandeputs', Anc., 4, Jan. 1903, p.29-43. See also 'The Vandeputs', Anc., 7, Oct., 1903, p.52-3.

BOSANQUET, N. E. T. 'The Vandeput family: an account given by Sir Peter Vandeput to his son J. V. at Amsterdam', Anc., 8, Jan., 1904, p.110-11.

WAKE

B[ARRON], O[swald], 'Our oldest families, I: Wake', Anc., 2, July 1902, p.109-13. [12-13th c.]

WANDESFORDE

'The Wandesfordes of Kirklington', Anc., 10, July 1904, p.98-103. [Yorkshire; 14-17th c.]

WATSON

See Monson-Watson

WIGTON

WILSON, James. 'Some extinct Cumberland families, I: the Wigtons', Anc., 3, Oct., 1902, p.73-80. [Pedigree, 12-14th c.]

WILMOT

'Genealogy of the family of Wilmot, Earls of Rochester', Anc., 11, Oct., 1904, p.15-25. [Oxfordshire; 16-17th c. pedigree]

'The wild Wilmots', Anc., 11, Oct., 1904, p.1-14. [16-17th c.]

WROTTESLEY

BARRON, Oswald. 'Our oldest families, IX: the Wrottesleys', Anc., 7, Oct., 1903, p.169-76. [Staffordshire; 12-19th c.]

WYNYARD

'A family of soldiers', Anc., 5, Apr. 1903, p.202f. [Wynyard pedigree, 18-19th c.]

2. GENEALOGICAL SOURCES

A. WILLS

BEWLEY, Edmund T. 'Original wills on parchment', Anc. 4, Jan. 1903, p.253-4. [Letter to the editor]

H., G. 'Four ancient English wills', Anc., 10, July 1904, p.13-21. [Robert Baran, [of London?], 1400; John Ryngfeld of London, 1439; Sir Thomas Latymer of Braybrook, 1402; Dame Anne Latymer, 1402]

H., G. 'Ten English wills from the Archdeaconry of London, 1400-1415', Anc., 5, Apr. 1903, p.159-66. [John Torell, 1400; Joan Coraunt, 1403; Richard Mymmes, 1404; Jonet Bylney, 1404; Henry Benet, 1407; Denys Benet, 1409; Agnes Spicer, 1410; John Hendy, 1412-13; Richard Edward, 1413; Piers Salle, 1415]

WITHINGTON, Lothrop. 'Will of Robert Devereux, Earl of Essex', Anc., 7, Oct., 1903, p.100-7. [of Chartleigh, Staffordshire]

B. OTHER

BURKE, H. Farnham. 'Some Cheshire deeds', Anc., 2, July 1902, p.129-47; 6, July 1903, p.19-45. [Abstracts of 201 deeds, 13-17th c.]

COX, J. Charles. 'The household book of Sir Miles Stapleton, Bart., 1656-1705', Anc., 2, July 1902, p.17-39 & 3, Oct., 1902, p.132-62. [Yorkshire]

COX, J. Charles. 'A parochial chartulary of the fourteenth century', Anc., 6, July 1903, p.103-18. [Crick, Derbyshire]

MALDEN, A. R. 'A Salisbury fifteenth century death register, 1467-75', Anc., 9, April 1904, p.28-35. [Deaths connected with the Cathedral]

RAGG, F. W. 'A charter of Gospatrik', Anc., 7, Oct., 1903, p.244-7. [Cumberland]

[ROUND, J. Horace]. 'Family history from private mss', Anc., 1, April 1902, p.258-64; 2, July 1902, p.197-204; 6, July 1903, p.92-102; 9, April 1904, p.6-19. [Notes from reports of the Historical Manuscripts Commission]

'Deeds relating to the family of Wydmerpol of Wydmerpol in Nottinghamshire', Anc., 10, July 1904, p.213-20. [27 deeds, 13-17th c.]

'A genealogist's kalendar of chancery suits of the time of Charles I', Anc., 1, April 1902, p.265-77, 2, July 1902, p.208-29; 3, Oct., 1902, p.49-72; 4, Jan., 1903, p.127-42; 5, Apr. 1903, p.81-91; 7, Oct., 1903, p.75-89; 9, April 1904, p.36-45; 11, Oct., 1904, p.161-9; 12, Dec., 1904, p.56-62.

3. HERALDRY

BAILDON, W. Pailey. 'Heralds' College and prescription', Anc., 8, Jan., 1904, p.113-44; 9, April 1904, p.214-24; 10, July 1904, p.52-69. See also letter by W. P. W. Phillimore, 5, April 1903, p.222-4. [Debate with anonymous author cited below, 'The prescriptive usage of arms']

BARRON, Oswald. 'Heraldry revived', Anc., 1, April 1902, p.36-57.

BARRON, Oswald. 'The genuinely armigerous person', Anc., 6, July 1903, p.155-74. See also letter by W. P. W. Phillimore, 7, Oct. 1903, p.267-8.

DORLING, E. E. 'Canting arms in the Zurich roll', Anc., 12, Dec., 1904, p.18-41.

DORLING, E. E. 'Fifteenth century heraldry', Anc., 12, Dec., 1904, p.146-8. [Tomb of Richard Metford, Bishop of Salisbury, 1407]

DORLING, E. E. 'Notes on two Nevill shields at Salisbury', Anc., 8, Jan., 1904, p.202-4.

DORLING, E. E. 'A Montagu shield at Hazelbury Bryan', Anc., 8, Jan., 1904, p.215-7. [Dorset]

FERRERS, Cecil S. F. 'The language of heraldry', Anc. 4, Jan. 1903, p.255. [Letter to the editor]

HALL, Hal. 'Notes on the tiles at Tewkesbury Abbey', Anc., 9, April 1904, p.46-64. [shewing coats of arms]

NEVILL, T. G. 'The evolution of the combed helmet', Anc., 3, Oct., 1902, p.87-92.

POYNTON, E. M. 'The change of seal of Gilbert de Clare', Anc., 2, July 1902, p.120.

ROTHERY, Guy Cadogan. 'The fleur-de-lis and its variations', Anc., 2, July 1902, p.99-106.

ROUND, J. Horace. 'The arms of the King-maker', Anc., 4, Jan., 1903, p.143-7; 5, Apr. 1903, p.195-202. See also letter from F. Hudlestone, Anc., 8, Jan. 1904, p.225-6. [i.e. Richard, Earl of Warwick; 15th c. With note by George Wrottesley]

SHEPARD, George. 'Shields from Clifton Reynes', Anc., 11, Oct., 1904, p.90-96. [Reynes family; Buckinghamshire]

VAN DE PUT, A. 'A note upon the arms attributed to Sir Hugh Calverley, Count of Carrion', Anc., 5, Apr. 1903, p.67-72.

WADE, W. Cecil. 'The rise of heraldry', Anc., 5, April, 1903, p.211-19 [Letter to the editor]

'A fifteenth century book of arms', Anc., 3, Oct., 1902, p.185-213 & 4, Jan., 1902, p.225-50; 5, Apr. 1903, p.175-90.

'A fifteenth century roll of arms', Anc., 7, Oct., 1903, p.184-215; 9, April 1904, p.159-80. See also letter by E. E. Dorling, Anc. 8, Jan. 1904, p.222.

'Friar Brackley's book of arms', Anc., 10, July 1904, p.87-97. [Mainly concerns the Paston family and thier allies, 15th c.]

'The prescriptive usage of arms', Anc., 2, July 1902,40-47. [See also article by Baildon cited above]

'The shield of arms on the tomb of Edmund of Langley', Anc., 2, July 1902, p.107. [Hertfordshire; d.1402]

'Thomas Wall's book of crests', Anc., 11, Oct., 1904, p.178-90, & Anc., 12, Dec., 1904, p.63-98. [16th c. compilation; includes index.]

4. GENERAL HISTORY AND GENEALOGY

BARRON, Oswald. 'The antiquary and the novelist', Anc., 5, Apr. 1903, p.54-65.

BARRON, Oswald. 'Arms and the Inland Revenue', Anc., 3, Oct., 1902, p.93-7. [Protest at the taxation of arms]

BARRON, Oswald. 'The twelfth volume of the Ancestor', Anc., 12, Dec., 1904, p.1-3.

BARRON, Mrs. Oswald, 'The journey of Gedeon Bonnivert to Ireland', Anc., 7, Oct., 1903, p.26-32. [Extract from a late 17th c. journal]

BIRD, W. H. B. 'Seals and arms', Anc., 10, July 1904, p.83-6.

BIRD, W. H. B. 'Whickleswick: a lost township', Anc., 4, Jan., 1902, p.205-24. [Descent of the township; now in Eccles, Lancashire]

LART, Charles E. 'Marguerite of Valois', Anc., 10, July 1904, p.22-31.

LART, Charles E. 'Some passive resisters of 1612', Anc., 12, Dec., 1904, p.104-10. [Huguenots at Norwich]

LINDSAY, W. A. 'Peerage cases', Anc., 1, April 1902, p.112-8.

MALDEN, A. R. 'An official account of the battle of Agincourt', Anc., 11, Oct., 1904, p.26-31.

MARSH, Bower. 'A tale of Bristol city', Anc., 7, Oct., 1903, p.90-99. [Chancery suit of Thomas Harvey of Bristol, 1684]

OBREEN, H. G. A. 'English forces in the Netherlands, A.D. 1396', Anc., 6, July 1903, p.135-6.

ROBINSON, J. C. 'The Westbury cup: an ancient scandal', Anc., 9, April 1904, p.187-90. [Wiltshire; 17th c. gift of a cup to Westbury church]

ROUND, J. Horace, MAXWELL-LYTE, Sir H., HOPE, W. H. St. John, & [BARRON, Oswald]. 'The barons' letter to the Pope', Anc., 6, July 1903, p.185-96; 7, Oct., 1903, p.248-59; 8, Jan., 1904, p.100-9. See also J. H. Round's comments in Anc., 12, Dec., 1904, p.166-8. [1301; includes notes on barons seals]

ROUND, J. Horace. 'Castle-guard', Anc., 6, July 1903, p.72-8.

ROUND, J. Horace. 'English counts of the Empire', Anc., 7, Oct., 1903, p.15-25. See also Anc. 9, April 1904, p.234.

ROUND, J. Horace. 'The Norman people: a retrospective review', Anc., 2, July 1902, p.165-74.

ROUND, J. Horace. 'The Lord Great Chamberlain case', Anc., 4, Jan., 1903, p.7-28. [Discussion of a legal case of 1902; includes pedigrees concerning various claimants to the office]

SCOTT, S. H. 'An ancient Scottish settlement in Hesse', Anc., 10, July 1904, p.70-72.

SITWELL, Sir George R. 'The English gentleman', Anc.,1, April 1902, p.58-103. See letters of J. Horace Round & 'A learned clerk', 2, July, 1902, p.230-4; of J. Horace Round & Aleyn Lyell Reade, Anc., 3, Oct. 1902, p.239-40; W. Paley Baildon. Anc., 7, Oct. 1903, p.261-2. [Origins of the gentry]

THOMPSON, F. D. 'Baronies by writ', Anc., 7, Oct. 1903, p.266. [Letter to the editor]

'VAN ---' [On the particle 'Van'], Anc., 3, Oct. 1902, p.237-8.

WOOD, H. J. T. 'The value of Welsh pedigrees', Anc., 4, Jan., 1903, p.47-60; 6, July 1903, p.62-5. See also letter from J. H. Round, Anc., 7, Oct. 1903, p.260-1. [Includes various Welsh medieval pedigrees]

'Editorial notes', Anc., 1, April 1902, p.278-82; 2, July 1902, p.236-43; 3, Oct., 1902, p.241-4; 4, Jan., 1902, p.258-66; 5, Apr. 1903, p.226-8; 6, July 1903, p.209-13; 7, Oct., 1903, p.269-73; 8, Jan., 1904, p.218-21; 9, April 1904, p.236-8; 10, July 1904, p.228-32; 11, Oct., 1904, p.201-6; 12, Dec., 1904, p.198-204.

'Letters to the editor', Anc., 2, July 1902, p.230-5; 3, Oct., 1902, p.241-4; 4, Jan., 1902, p.251-7; 5, Apr. 1903, p.211-25; 6, July 1903, p.206-8; 7, Oct., 1903, p.260-8; 8, Jan., 1904, p.222-32; 9, April 1904, p.234-5; 10, July 1904, p.221-7; 11, Oct., 1904, p.197-200; 12, Dec., 1904, p.188-97.

'What is believed', Anc., 1, April 1902, p.226-42, 2, July 1902, p.187-96; 3, Oct., 1902, p.118-26; 4, Jan., 1902, p.183-8; 5, Apr. 1903, p.138-47; 6, July 1903, p.148-54; 7, Oct., 1903, p.177-83; 8, Jan., 1904, p.205-14; 9, April 1904, p.150-8; 10, July 1904, p.138-44; 11, Oct., 1904, p.170-7; 12, Dec., 1904, p.178-85.

5. ART

BARRETT-LENNARD, Thomas. 'The family pictures at Belhus', Anc., 5, Apr. 1903, p.1-18. [Essex]

BARRON, Oswald. 'Costume at the end of the middle ages', Anc., 12, Dec., 1904, p.125-42.

BARRON, Oswald. 'Early fourteenth century costume', Anc., 8, Jan., 1904, p.145-66.

BARRON, Oswald. 'Fifteenth century costume', Anc., 9, April 1904, p.113-36, & 10, July 1904, p.120-32.

DORLING, E. E. 'Notes on some armorial glass in Salisbury Cathedral', Anc., 4, Jan., 1903, p.120-6.

HOPE, W. H. St. John. 'The King's coronation ornaments', Anc., 1, April 1902, p.127-59, & 2, July 1902, p.63-81.

HYLTON, Lord. 'The story of a key', Anc., 4, Jan., 1903, p.44-6. See also letter by Frances C. Baldwyn Childe, 5, April 1903, p.219-20. [Concerning the 17th c. portrait of Thomas Jolliffe; Staffordshire]

LAKING, Guy Francis. 'Swords from the Morgan Williams collection', Anc., 2, July 1902, p.124-8.

LONGE, Julia G. 'The purse of the Great Seal in 1578', Anc., 6, July 1903, p.119-20.

MANNERS, Victoria Lady. 'The miniatures at Belvoir', Anc., 1, April 1902, p.28-356.

NATHAN, G. E. 'Some portraits at the Society of Antiquaries', Anc., 2, July 1902, p.14-16; 3, Oct., 1902, p.41-8; 4, Jan., 1902, p.190-204; 6, July 1903, p.79-88.

'English costume of the early fourteenth century', Anc., 7, Oct., 1903, p.108-36.

'Pictures of English dress in the thirteenth century', Anc., 5, Apr. 1903, p.99-137.

'St. George and the dragon', Anc., 8, Jan., 1904, p.112. [Carving on bench-end]

6. REVIEWS

A. REVIEW ARTICLES

BAILDON, W. Pailey. 'North country wills', Anc., 4, 1903, p.101-14. [Reviews of COLLINS, Francis, ed. Wills and administrations from the Knaresborough court rolls, vol.1, and CLAY, J. W., ed. Testamenta Eboracensis: a selection of wills from the Registry at York, vol. 6.]

LEGG, L. Wickham. 'The coronation: three books, and a protest', Anc., 1, April 1902, p.220-5. [Reviews of PEMBERTON, Joseph H. The Coronation service according to the use of the Church of England, EELES, F. C. The coronation service: its teaching and history, and MACLEANE, Douglas. The great solemnity of the coronation of the king and queen of England.]

B. INDIVIDUAL REVIEWS

ARMITAGE-SMITH, Sydney. John of Gaunt. [Oswald Barron]. Anc., 12, Dec., 1904, p.143-5..

BARNARD, Francis Pierrepont. The companion to English history. Anc., 2, July 1902, p.156-9.

BENHAM, W. Gurney. The red paper book of Colchester. [J. Horace Round]. Anc., 4, Jan., 1902, p.149-51.

BEWLEY, Sir Edmund Thomas. The Bewleys of Cumberland. [Oswald Barron]. Anc., 4, Jan., 1902, p.176-82.

BEWLEY, Sir Edmund T. Some notes on the Lowthers who held judicial office in Ireland in the seventeenth century. Anc., 2, July 1902, p.163-4.

BLACKER, Latham C. M. A history of the family of Blackers of Carrickblacker in Ireland. Anc.,9, April 1904, p.105-12.

BRENAN, Gerald. A history of the house of Percy. Anc., 3, Oct., 1902, p.229-36

BULLOCH, J. M., ed. The house of Gordon. [Oswald Barron]. Anc., 9, April 1904, p.89-102.

CURWEN, John F. Curwen pedigree. Anc., 9, April 1904, p.225-9. [of Workington]

DAVIES, Randall. Chelsea old church. Anc., 10, July 1904, p.145-6.

DOYLE, A. Conan. The White company. [Oswald Barron]. Anc., 3, Oct., 1902, p.177-8. See reply by Conan Doyle, Anc. 4, Jan. 1903, p.251-3.

DUNKIN, ed. Sussex marriage licences. [J. Horace Round]. Anc., 4, Jan., 1902, p.170-1.

FANING, J. F. E. The book of matriculations and degrees: a catalogue of those who have been matriculated or admitted to any degree in the University of Cambridge from 1851 to 1900. Anc., 7, Oct., 1903, p.148.

FARRER, William. A history of the parish of North Meols ... [Oswald Barron]. Anc., 7, Oct., 1903, p.142-7 [Lancashire]

FARRER, William. Lancashire pipe rolls. [J. Horace Round]. Anc., 4, Jan., 1902, p.151-9.

FINCH, Pearl. History of Burley-on-the-Hill, Rutland. Anc., 2, July 1902, p.160-2.

FOSTER, Joseph. Some feudal coats of arms. [Oswald Barron], Anc., 1, April 1902, p.207-18. See also Anc., 12, Dec., 1904, p.156-65.

GEORGE, Major. Pedigrees and history of the families of George and Gorges. [Oswald Barron]. Anc., 9, April 1904, p.83-8.

HAWTREY, Florence Molesworth. The history of the Hawtrey family. Anc., 12, Dec., 1904, p.99-103.

HIGGINS, Napier. The Bernards of Abington and Nether Winchendon. Anc., 7, Oct., 1903, p.149-62.

HITCHIN-KEMP, Frederick. A general history of the Kemp and Kempe families. Anc., 5, Apr. 1903, p.148-54.

HOPE, W. H. St. John. Stall plates of the Knights of the Garter. Anc., 3, Oct., 1902, p.163-6.

HUTTON, Alfred, The sword and the centuries. [Oswald Barron] Anc., 4, Jan., 1902, p.166-9.

MADAN, Falconer. The Gresleys of Drakelow. [J. Horace Round] Anc., 1, April 1902, p.195-202.

MAXWELL, Sir Horace. A history of the house of Douglas. [Sir George Douglas] Anc., 1, April 1902, p.203-6.

METCALFE, John Henry. A great historic peerage: the Earldome of Wiltes. Anc., 4, Jan., 1902, p.173-6. [Scrope family of Danby]

NEILSON, George. Huchown of the awle ryale, the alliterative poet. Anc., 2, July 1902, p.159-60.

PHILLIMORE, W. P. W. Some account of the family of Middlemore of Warwickshire and Worcestershire. [Oswald Barron]. Anc., 7, Oct., 1903, p.33-44. See also reply by Phillimore, 9, April 1904, p.230-3.

RAINES, Francis Robert. Life of Humphrey Chetham ... [W. H. B. Bird]. Anc., 8, Jan., 1904, p.82-99.

ROBINSON, John. The Attwood family. [Oswald Barron]. Anc., 9, April 1904, p.137-45. See also letter from Thos. A. C. Attwood. Anc. 10, July 1904, p.221-3.

SHADWELL, Charles Lancelot. Registrum Orielense. Anc., 4, Jan., 1902, p.159-61.

WEDDERBURN, Alexander Dundas Ogilvy. The Wedderburn book: a history of Wedderburns in the counties of Berwick and Forfar, etc. Anc., 5, Apr. 1903, p.155-8; 6. July 1903, p.49-61.

WOLLASTON, G. Woods. Coronation of King Edward VII: the Court of Claims: cases and evidence. [W. Paley Baildon]. Anc., 7, Oct., 1903, p.137-41.

WROTTESLEY, George. The Giffards. Anc., 3, Oct., 1902, p.223-8.

Almanack de Gotha. [Oswald Barron]. Anc., 9, April 1904, p.103-4.

Calendar of the close rolls preserved in the Public Record Office. [J. Horace Round]. Anc., 1, April 1902, p.243-57; 4, Jan., 1903, p.148.

Calendar of the Patent Rolls preserved in the Public Record Office. Henry IV. [J. Horace Round]. Anc., 7, Oct., 1903, p.163-5.

Descriptive catalogue of ancient deeds in the Public Record Office. [J. Horace Round]. Anc., 6, July 1903, p.175-84.

An exact list of the Lords spiritual and temporal. Anc., 4, Jan., 1902, p.171-3.

Imperial heraldic kalendar 1903. Anc., 4, Jan., 1902, p.161-5.

Scottish heraldic kalendar for the year 1902. Anc., 4, Jan., 1902, p.161-5.

The story of the Stewarts. [J. Horace Round]. Anc., 1, April 1902, p.218-9.

Wiltshire notes and queries. Anc., 6, July 1903, p.203-5.

AUTHOR INDEX

This index does not include authors of books reviewed; it does, however, include authors of reviews.

INDEX OF FAMILY NAMES

INDEX OF PLACES

ENGLAND

UNIDENTIFIED

OVERSEAS